The Libertine's Progress

The Libertine's Progress

SEDUCTION IN THE EIGHTEENTH-CENTURY FRENCH NOVEL

Pierre Saint-Amand

Translated by Jennifer Curtiss Gage

BROWN UNIVERSITY PRESS

Published by University Press of New England • Hanover and London

Brown University Press
Published by University Press of New England, Hanover, NH 03755

Printed in the United States of America
5 4 3 2 1
CIP data appear at the end of the book

CONTENTS

FOREWORD

Among the distinctive achievements of modern French culture, none is greater, I believe, than a certain type of essay. . . . No, I am not thinking of Montaigne. His exuberance and capriciousness are marvellous, but the works I have in mind are different.

The French often refer to them as *essais classiques*, with the stress on the second word, to emphasize these traits, precisely, for which the founder of the genre is not especially noted—self-discipline, simplicity, and, above all, singleness of purpose.

The classical label is not intended to suggest that the *essai classique* is historically rooted in the so-called classical age. It really comes later. Its great period begins with the nineteenth century and is not over yet. This golden age coincides with the reign of nihilism. The authors of these essays are no nihilists, however. In a world where thinking is disdained unless it can be turned into money or political propaganda, they celebrate and cultivate apparently "useless" ideas, although in a highly selective fashion. Ideas should never be celebrated en masse, as if all of them were necessarily equal. This attitude is the benevolent side of nihilism, and it is just as bad as an open contempt for all ideas.

Many people try to escape nihilism by retreating into the past through the sheer force of nostalgia, but it cannot be done and they become bitter. The authors of classical essays successfully escape nihilism. They are not particularly nostalgic or even hostile to the world in which they live. They understand its historical raison d'être too well.

Unlike most people around them, they see nihilism as a particular creed that they cannot espouse. In a certain sense, therefore, they are more nihilistic than everybody else, but in another sense they are not. They believe in the power not of ideas in general but of some very specific ideas. It is not a matter of faith with them but of experience. They think that they have personally experienced the power of these ideas.

These ideas, they have discovered, generate too much coherence and significance, in too many areas, to be treated as ordinary. Exciting and even exhilarating as this discovery may be, it is not mystical in the slightest. It is an intellectual and therefore eminently communicable experience.

All real ideas, however, are somewhat complex and delicate. In order to be fully appreciated and evaluated, they demand a quality of attention that, sadly enough, books no longer command in our world, even in academic circles. There are too many of them, perhaps. Paradoxically, the devaluation of language leads to a monstrous proliferation of books.

Even if a book is lucky enough to attract some attention, it is unlikely that it will receive the serious examination that all authors inevitably crave and that very few genuinely deserve. If the ideas in a book are not shrugged off as the by-product of some banal family trauma or of sordid class interest, they will be made a part of some historical sequence, they will be regarded as mere rearrangements of earlier ideas.

Thinking is highly encouraged in universities, and it gets everything it needs except what it needs most, the generous and unprejudiced attention of people genuinely interested in it. Far from occurring in an age of disbelief, our nihilism is a great condensation of belief, although entirely focused only on those ideas that seek the destruction of all other ideas.

Is our tired world still willing to give disinterested intelligence a chance? This question cannot fail to weigh heavily on the mind of would-be authors. They are at the mercy of readers whose attention span is very brief and whose good will is quickly exhausted. Their chances of being heard are few and they do not want to squander them.

If would-be authors are courageous enough to assess the

intellectual situation correctly, and if, above all, they have something significant to say, they will conclude that their only viable course is the most direct and simple approach, the strategy of the job well done and of the most effective prose. Our courageous would-be authors will be too committed to their ideas not to shun the sensationalism to which many desperate people resort nowadays, and they will try to write an *essai classique*. This is what Pierre Saint-Amand has done, and he has succeeded.

He has chosen the strategy of no strategy at all. Not a word in his book is superfluous; not a turn of phrase is selected for rhetorical effect. That is why he writes so elegantly. Good writing always is the product of harsh circumstances. It is somewhat consoling to think that the skeptical lassitude of the present and its indifference to intellectual values must have made a contribution, if only an indirect one, to the luminous display of intelligence and sensibility that this little book represents.

However, I should not dramatize the writing of this essay too much; I might convey the impression that Pierre Saint-Amand is a tense and beleaguered author, and he is nothing of the sort. He is perfectly at ease with his theme, seduction in the eighteenth-century novel; he writes about it with all the deftness and lightness appropriate to the subject.

His major approach, true enough, is controversial. I am in a good position to realize that *mimetic desire* is not universally popular in our humanistic fields. For some reason, Pierre Saint-Amand easily eludes the dogmaticism to which an interest in mimetic desire is supposed to make us vulnerable. He often resorts to psychoanalytical ideas, for instance, and with remarkable results. Where some people see rigid oppositions, he discovers avenues of contact, and he pursues them efficiently and rapidly, never belaboring his points, yet never so hasty either as to betray the spirit of the various perspectives that he manages to reconcile.

The novels that Saint-Amand studies reproduce in fainter, yet perfectly recognizable, outline the mimetic patterns characteristic of myth and tragedy. These patterns are not lifeless vestiges or even static themes but the very form of the human relations that unfold in the novels, the most visible signs of mimetic processes that also make themselves manifest in other ways, in the dramatic details of these works, of course, as well as in their overall plots.

The vicissitudes of seduction and sexual affairs are governed by the laws of the model/obstacle (*skandalon*), the mimetic doubles, pseudonarcissism, the sacrificial crisis, and the transferential runaway against a single victim, or "scapegoat mechanism." In novel after novel, new aspects of these schemes are uncovered, and, as the crisis of which they are a part intensifies, they undergo various transformations that tend to reproduce diachronically the logic of the mimetic process.

The approach provides an umbrella under which the proximity, even unity, of certain phenomena that traditional perspectives found difficult to reconcile, become self-evident. This is the case, for instance, at the end of the century in question, with the growing fascination with the occult, often judged "paradoxical" in the context of Enlightenment rationalism. From a mimetic standpoint, hypnosis, magnetism, mesmerism, and so on are by-products of the same crisis that is also signified by the increasingly violent, promiscuous, and demonic turn that seduction takes at the very end of the century, notably in Laclos and Sade.

As it substitutes the continuous logic of its crisis for the discontinuities of literary history, the mimetic perspective dissolves certain traditional problems, automatically reinterpreting them as misunderstandings rooted in standard philosophical attitudes.

Pierre Saint-Amand restores to their rightful place the various catastrophes that occur in the conclusions of many novels. When modernist ideology minimizes the punishment of villains, in these novels, it resists the ancient pull of mythical scapegoat transference, and this attitude would be praiseworthy, to be sure, if it were not motivated primarily by an inverted moralism even less able to question its own sacrificial nature than the standard moralism that it replaces.

The modernism that would censor Madame de Merteuil's

smallpox out of *Les Liaisons dangereuses* and hell itself out of *Don Giovanni* truly reduces the drama of eighteenth-century seduction to the pornographic consumerism that, judging from our contemporary disintegration, must have been its manifest destiny all along. The suppression of the tragic dimension flatters the temper of our time, and that is why the "reductionism" implicit in it is never condemned, never even perceived. Ironically, critics obsessed with reductionism tend to focus their accusations primarily on the perspective that restores the structural wholeness of the works they study, the mimetic perspective.

This essay spectacularly refuses the bizarre belief, reinforced by deconstruction and postmodernism, according to which respect for diversity must be bought at the price of unity. Far from hindering the deployment of difference, the mimetic scheme enables the critic to articulate singularities by revealing in them variations on the same mimetic patterns at different stages in their isolation. Critical insights form a rich network of correspondences around an organizing principle that is truly the vital center of the essay.

This last statement should raise an outcry. A universally valid principle of unity is what our contemporary world has learned to regard as an impossibility. This is the number-one rule of our "postmetaphysical" world. I believe in it myself, but I never forget that the rule applies only to *metaphysically* grounded principles.

Is mimetic desire a metaphysically grounded principle of unity? Those who distrust it swear that it is, of course, but their acquaintance with it is invariably limited to its most superficial and banal applications. When handled as powerfully as in the present essay, mimetic desire becomes a deconstructive tool not only of the human relations directly analyzed but also of the conceptual apparatus that goes with them.

Far from being a metaphysical center, the mimetic scheme is the decentering operation par excellence. It reaches all aspects of the work, because it radiates from the former metaphysical center. What unseats this former center is the discovery of the nonmetaphysical origin in which all metaphysical systems of representation are grounded, the transference of the unanimous victim system, the "scapegoat mechanism."

When we really get hold of this decentering centrality, we can write coherently once again about the presumed incoherence of desire and language. The idea that our culture is irreducibly chaotic and cannot be criticized effectively unless the critics and their texts manage to impersonate chaos is a remarkably naive reassumption of the mimetic stance by those who wish they could wish it away, a residue of the old avant-garde. As long as we try to get rid of mimetic desire merely by pretending that it is not there, we will turn ourselves into the living proof of its continued dominance.

The reason why the mimetic scheme causes anxiety and resentment in some circles is that it pushes demythification beyond the reaches of our purely humanistic culture, into the religious area that is the key to our current cultural impasse. It thus violates the most powerful taboo of modernism, which is the exclusion of the religious. There is no worse *reductionism* than the reduction of the religious to the extreme superficiality of *superstition*.

Saint-Amand defines the ultimate goal of mimetic desire as self-divinization, divine self-sufficiency. The traditional name of the structures generated by this rivalry with God is Satan. The return of the satanic in the late eighteenth-century novel should not scare the living daylights out of our humanists. When humanism was still alive, there were humanistic interpretations of Satan, and it is this essay's *coup de genie* that it concludes with the greatest one, which is also the most fitting one from a historical and cultural standpoint.

It concludes with Goethe's great explication with Satan, *Faust*, and this conclusion is immediately preceded by an analysis of *Elective Affinities*, Goethe's great explication with mimetic desire.

Taken all together in chronological order, the novels studied in this essay seem to constitute a single novel that has the same form as each of these components. Between the Regency and the Revolution, this ideal novel reenacts the whole mimetic process with the Terror in the role of the victim-making mechanism and with Goethe, later, embodying an ambiguous rebirth of the cultural order.

It may be objected, of course, that the small group of novels selected for this study represent chiefly the choice of posterity, the so-called literary *canon*. Why not? Insofar as it is true—and up to a point it must be true—this idea can only suggest that mimetic and sacrificial considerations must play a role, perhaps the principal role, in the canonization of certain works in preference to others.

This preference in turn must reflect an obscure realization that history itself in that period should reenact the mimetic process. Our view of eighteenth-century French history is inseparable from a crisis and catharsis pattern that culminates in the Revolution and its Napoleonic aftermath.

With his Goethean conclusion, Pierre Saint-Amand makes this form esthetically and intellectually perfect. His last chapter is a discreet, yet powerful, homage to German classicism and the unity of European culture. No other writer but Goethe could provide a nonreligious, a still humanistic summation of what Pierre Saint-Amand's *essai classique* is about.

RENÉ GIRARD

ACKNOWLEDGMENTS

This book, written during the tenure of a fellowship at the Stanford Humanities Center in 1985–86, originally appeared in France under the title *Séduire ou la passion des Lumières* (Paris: Méridiens-Klincksieck, 1987). It has been substantially revised and expanded for this American edition. I would like to thank my colleagues at Stanford, Bliss Carnochan and Herbert Lindenberger, for their encouragement of my work. I express my gratitude to Zakiya Hanafi for translating a first version of this book and to Eric Clarke for his continuous support and friendship. I would also like to thank Brown University for providing financial support for this translation and finally, in a very special way, Jennifer Gage for her untiring meticulousness, her precision, and her generous complicity. I could not have dreamt of a more refined translator. Jennifer's inexhaustible language truly made this translation a radical improvement on the original.

P. ST.-A.

The Libertine's Progress

Introduction

The Mirrored Bedroom

The eighteenth century, Baudrillard tells us, witnessed the twilight of seduction. Its flights of passion, elaborate arabesques of gallantry, and unabashed libertinage are still evoked with nostalgia. As Baudrillard writes, "The eighteenth century still spoke of seduction. It was, with valour and honour, a central preoccupation of the aristocratic spheres."[1] But seduction, I would argue, must be apprehended somewhat closer to its origin. It is above all fascination, mesmerism, sorcery. My interest, then, lies in the magic of magnetic gestures, in the intimidation of the gaze that transfixes.

Enlightenment novels are peopled with hordes of seducers. It is not enough to trace in their gestures the stamp of the libertine code; we must also probe the diabolical intent of their gaze. Beneath the flaunted gallantry, the libertine flourish of these novels, a profoundly archaic core can be found lurking in the shadows of metaphor. Modernity chafes at this archaic residue, which it cannot efface. Yet, this archaism is itself an allegorical form of desire, the mask desire dons when it seems to relegate to the distant past the relations of those who succumb, in our day, to its law. Archaism is the hypocritical form of an abiding pulse of desire: it is desire's archetype. The eighteenth century—devoted, as we know, to libertine superficiality—needed this ancient decor in order to surprise us by showing that it, too, was haunted by the dark side of Desire.

I propose to read the eighteenth-century novel as the locus

in which the so-called Enlightenment reveals its underside, foundering on the blind reefs of desire. Atheistic philosophers (except perhaps Diderot) have no place in this world of obscure desires and ancient fears. Their place is taken by creatures of the night under the spell of Evil. My aim is to restore all their satanic excess to these beings from another century—as if the libertine parade, the rhetoric of love, and the apparent game of seduction concealed in broad daylight these bewigged monsters, these sirens and bacchantes. Such words are not mere metaphors; they reveal the terror of seduction in the novels, and they tell the truth about a century that still believed in its superstitions.

For the eighteenth-century novel—this bears repeating—is superstitious. It can be read as the unconscious, as a palimpsest of all the atheistic philosophies of the Age of Reason. Seduction reigns, indeed, but as an avatar of archaic fears. Sade locates the origin of the novel in imaginary seduction and in superstition: "Everything was a novel, because the gods spoke only through the medium of men who, more or less interested in this ridiculous artifice, did not fail to make up the language of phantoms, from whatever they imagined would be most likely to seduce or terrify."[2]

Love in the novel occupies the place of the cult of divinity and ancient religious practices. In this sense the novel is always idolatrous: "Man," writes Sade, "is prey to two weaknesses. . . . Wheresoever on earth he dwells, man feels the need *to prey*, and *to love*: and herein lies the basis for all novels" (99). The seductive relation that binds novelistic characters is more than a game: it is a spell-binding, a supernatural bond(age). These characters must not be denied their mythological status: Medusa, Delilah, the Gorgon, and the Devil are a few of their forgotten metamorphoses.

Within this population we must distinguish between coquettes and seducers. As rivals in desire, they share a place in this gallant inferno. The coquette appears in these novels as one of the modern figures of sorcery. Despite the widely held belief that witches had been expelled from the Age of Enlightenment and packed off far from the shores of Reason, along with their craft,[3] the eighteenth-century novel brings the sorceress back into our phantasms, back within the horizon of our desires. Her secrets, her ability to hypnotize the other through her enticing attire, her rites of initiation are all terrifying: once again, the witch is back with her charms, potions, and poisons.

In the imaginary of the social collective, we must understand the coquette as the modern construction of the sorceress. In Sade, the coquette reigns like a high priestess amidst her bottles and vials, her aphrodisiacs. Prévost imbues the coquette with an enchanting scent; her presence alone electrifies. Marivaux, timid and chaste, nevertheless delivers Marianne fully coiffed and thus endows his orphan with singular virtues. She, too, bewitches her targets, seeing into the deepest secrets of their souls. The coquette is above all a soothsayer, endowed with superhuman talents. Her beauty isolates her from the community; she can multiply herself at will, take on various faces, and refuse to give herself to anyone. The persecuting voice of public rumor loses no time in condemning her to trial by calumny. As a foreigner to the community that takes her in—she is orphaned, abducted from home, torn from her obscure past (Marianne, Manon, Suzanne Simonin)—she wields redoubled powers of fascination.

As for the seducer—what is he but the Devil with a modern face and wordly tastes? His modern development must be traced through the flurry of imposture that characterized the eighteenth century, played out against the backdrop of occult practices in vogue at the time. As Jean-Didier Vincent admirably sums it up, "the eighteenth century is the century of imposture."[4] Mesmer, Cagliostro, Saint-Germain, and Casanova were the great heroes of seduction during this period.[5] Each in his way possessed the same secrets of the soul and the same hypnotic powers. The public bowed down before them as they did before their God. Mesmer, wielding his phallic wand, played at Orpheus for society ladies.

The rakes that people eighteenth-century novels keep company with soothsayers and fortune-tellers. The libertines received their magical powers from the community and frequented the bedrooms of palm-readers. The Sadean seducer is modeled after these charlatans; the political fate of Sade's libertines is based on such fantastical characters.

All we need do to get a clear view of the eighteenth century is to lift up the veil of Reason. Distinctions already begin to blur between Sade's boudoirs of torture and Mesmer's "*crisis rooms*," where women succumbed to delirium by contagion.[6] It is hardly surprising that Sade and Goethe were Freemasons, that Casanova kept company with the Marquise d'Urfé, both a libertine and a witch, that Diderot abandoned his *Encyclopédie* to write a diabolical novel, or that Valmont's seduction in *Les Liaisons dangereuses* is so magnetically charged with the technics of seduction that were all the rage at the time. Nerval's *Illuminés* reminded us of the murky depths that lay beneath the Age of Reason. Yet, his book was eclipsed by his romanticism, by the allegorical diabolism of the nineteenth century. "Books on the Cabbalah and occult sciences flooded collections," he reminded us.[7] A whole literature on the Cabbalah flourished within easy reach of the salons. The *Illuminés* could be read as a refashioning of this library of superstitions. Enlightenment/Illuminism: the antisuperstitious psychosis of the eighteenth century must be read in the kinship between these two terms, in the reversibility of this complementary coupling.

Closer to us, Michel Foucault was well aware of these archaic aspects of the eighteenth-century novel. He also realized that these archaisms cover up a general metaphorization of desire: "Most eighteenth-century novels . . . are full of insidious poisonous preparations: camphor, snakeskins, powdered turtledove bones, and above all, the terrible Javanese ant-eggs. Finally, there is the inoculation against inadmissible desires that trouble the hearts of the most faithful: illusory delights, true pleasures. All those nonmagical philters."[8]

We must appreciate the true potency of all these philters. Yet I intend to go even further. Not only will I insist on rousing the ghosts that haunt the eighteenth century, on stirring up their ashes to infuse them with a breath of truth; what I wish to show through the novels of the eighteenth century—by describing the mechanisms of desire and the interrelations to which beings are subjected by this desire—is that century's superstitious core.

Narcissus-Lucifer

> Par le regard, je touche,
> j'atteins, je saisis, je suis saisi.
> —BARTHES[9]

I would like to examine these intricacies of desire against the backdrop of a genealogy of seduction in order to avoid a typology that would catalog and classify the seducers according to their successes and failures, freezing their appearance and their qualities. Typology might be said to strip the seducer of his desire, turning his seduction into a banal mechanism. Leporello counts, while Don Giovanni sings his desire at the top of his lungs. . . .

The vital link in this genealogy is the desire for seduction itself; that is, the genealogy takes desire as a structural, evolutionary figure and, in a somewhat Kierkegaardian maneuver, follows the trajectory from its obscure birth (desire wrapped up in itself, so to speak) all the way to its theoretical (intellectual) explosion. At this point of arrival, desire recognizes its object not in its victim but in its reflexive *jouissance*. This moment of theoretical solitude, which Kierkegaard sees as the *erotic* (or *intensive*) moment proper to seduction, is perhaps also the moment of the most absolute attraction. Yet this ecstasy of desire is precarious; the seducer can end up a victim of Desire.[10] As John Forrester succinctly puts it: "The seducer may turn him- or herself into the seduced, by introducing into the other a passion which then overwhelms him."[11] The present genealogy follows more closely the path marked out by René Girard when he speaks of a progressive, reflexive aggravation of desire: "Desire is always using for its own ends the knowledge it has acquired of itself. . . . Desire bears light, but puts that light in the service of its own darkness; it places the truth in the service of its own untruth."[12]

We will observe the entangled progression of this desire from Marivaux to Goethe, appreciating in each seduction the quality of desire that informs it. The names of the characters who play out these episodes are of little importance; they are but stages in the progression of desire. I will attempt to show how an episode of seduction contains in embryonic form the elements of a more elaborate seduction. By thus unraveling seductive desire, we will be better able to grasp the complexity and wealth of its component parts, its progressive theorization, and the delirious pretension of its aims.

In this study, seduction operates around a principle figure: that of *mediation*, with reference to René Girard's notion of mimetic desire. Paisley Livingston offers a simple and elegant definition of the phenomenon in *Models of Desire: René Girard and the Psychology of Mimesis*:

> René Girard refers to mimetic desire as *le désir selon l'Autre*, "desire according to the other." He contrasts mimetic desire to desire *selon soi*, desire that is a spontaneous and autonomous manifestation of an individual's inherent wants or preferences. Instead of having an "immediate" relation to his or her objects of desire, the person who desires mimetically has a "mediated" relation to them, one that takes a detour through a model. Desire, then, is said to be "triangular," for its most basic structure involves at least three terms: the agent who desires, the object of this agent's desire, and the agent who serves as the "model" or "mediator" of the desire.[13]

Seductive mediation offers a particular structure: it is always internal. By that I mean, in Girard's terms, that the model of desire installs himself in the closest proximity to the desiring subject. The relation between model and agent is not dependent on sociological hierarchy; it is primarily spiritual. The content of seduction always involves some degree of emulation. The seducee's selection of the seducer implies what Paisley Livingston calls "tutelary beliefs," beliefs that involve "the mimetic agent's view that the model's desire corresponds to an intrinsically superior choice"; "tutelary beliefs are beliefs that inform the believer that someone's desires are worth copying."[14] This means that the mediating seducer, feigning external mediation, can imitate a transcendental quality (autonomy, self-sufficiency, in a word *Being*). Hence the veneration, the idolatry that he provokes in the other. The seducer wants to be Desire for the other; he wants to stand in the place of the other's desire, *fascinans* and *fascinum*, obstacle and rival at the same time.

The seducer is the model of the other's desire, but he also becomes the object of the other's desire. He usurps the place of the object, assimilating it to his being. Internal mediation performs this reduction (with respect to the triangular model), bringing the subject of desire closer to the mediator; that is, internal mediation is a step toward the true destination of desire. Becoming a rival for the other's passion, the seducer dazzles the other with a blinding light. Seduction is a strategic military *occupation*. In the female form of the tantalizing coquette, or in the male form of the seducer who initiates, we find the same tendency of desire. The seducer points us toward the royal road of desire, but he places himself jealously on the horizon, like a beacon, both shimmering mirage and obstacle.

On the part of the seduced there is a tendency to absolutize the seducer as model. The model becomes for the seduced the sole executor of the privilege of desire. Seduction arouses in the self the desire for the other. Lurking in the silent pact of seduction is the deceitful "promise of metaphysical autonomy," the ontological delusion of which Girard speaks.[15] The person who is seduced seeks his lost divinity in the other, desperately believing that he will be able to recover this "divine heritage." Inside seduction slumbers a sort of *religiosity* of desire: the term comes from Daniel Sibony, who sees seduction as a "playful, sometimes exasperated quest for an object-god to consume."[16] Michèle Bertrand perfectly sums up the dilemma of seduction when she writes that "To seduce is to become master of the other's desire, to forbid him to be desiring. . . . To be seduced is to allow oneself to be enslaved by the other's desire, in order to have nothing left to desire."[17]

Seductive mediation choreographs this potent lure to which

both partners fall victim. Reflecting the same desire to each other, they are stifled by the same lack. This would explain the double meaning of seduction both as a leading astray by the other's influence and as charm or enchantment. This mimetic tendency is projected as the other's hold over the subject, which charm both aggravates and "confounds." To return to the inversion of positions in the seductive relationship, which I have already mentioned, one might say that the model of desire can himself be carried away by that to which he is supposed to direct the other. Through the agency of the person seduced, the seducer can become infected by the contagion of seduction, in which case he imitates the desire initially offered to the other; the process of seduction would thus make the partners *doubles* of each other.[18]

Mimicry

If the seducer assumes the diabolical figure of the sorcerer in the novels we are about to examine, it is because he is able to induce unanimity of desire in others. His knowledge of desire accords him a privileged, yet isolated, position in the community. Mauss's description of the magician might be applied to the seducer: "he is a being who has believed himself and who has at the same time put himself in the position of being believed and being viewed as unparalleled by the rest."[19] He acquires his power only by being the best imitator of his initiators (by mimicking gestures, rites, and sensations). Casanova knew this very well when he confided that "Sorcerers have never existed in this world, but their power has always existed in those who had the talent to make themselves believed as such."[20] The initiations that take place in Enlightenment novels must be read in this context of wizardry and hocus-pocus. In Crébillon's *The Wayward Head and Heart*, Versac takes aside his pupil Meilcour and asks him to observe the utmost secrecy with regard to his lessons in the art of seducing.

Whereas the male seducer's initiation ends in the verbal utterance of a certain knowledge, female initiation, in contrast, strikes the subject in an instant flash of knowledge: it is fatal. The coquette can appear as the very type of maleficent seduction, yet only inasmuch as she arouses excessive desire. If the seductress trails all her philters and charms with her, it is because she knows the secret lures and traps of desire. But more important, it is in her narcissism that desire loses its way and finds it most powerful rival. In this sense, the coquette perfectly fulfills the double role of internal mediation. She is its most accomplished artist: the more she offers herself as an invitation to desire, the more she ultimately refuses to take part in her games of desire. The mirror in which her coquetry shines, in which she adorns her self-importance, is the best artifice of her terrifying power. And it is this knowledge about desire that renders her scandalous. The seductress, too, has her own models. She emulates the mythical figures of bewitchment: Delilah, Medusa, Venus.

Sade's novels, taking internal mediation to its extreme, multiply seducers through the contagion of desire. The refractory mimesis that affects Sade's characters verges on the most liminal regions. To illustrate the negative evolution of desire, Sade reduces it to its primitive animal predecessors. Sadean desire shows the intensity of the seducer's vow to appropriate the other, as well as the depth of his lack (hence the absorption in orgies in the search for totalization). The mask that Sade erects is unable to conceal this truth about desire. I maintain that Sade's work seeks an impossible mimetic coincidence with the other (desire for possession, for resemblance, for absorption) but at the same time rejects it as "inadmissible." This specular confrontation takes place with the disciple, but it is multiplied, almost made banal, by the passivity of the victims.

Mimetic confrontation also reaches its limits in Sade. His teachers are immoral mediators whose desire for appeasement is never satisfied. Victims and disciples multiply in a proselytism that is essentially imitative corruption. This saturation of the mimetic space affects not only the erotic scene but also the libertine's famous "dissertations." The resounding echo of his words is meant to glut his senses. The ritual of speech, the deafening repetition of his principles, takes on the power of mimetic conviction. His goal is not only to eroticize the partner but also to occupy the space of that other's consciousness or, even better, as Sade conceived it, to saturate his imagination, the sublime locus of all his passions. The dissertating voice of the libertine hypnotizes the disciple. Through this sort of erotic suggestion, the libertine model dazes his listener. Barthes was well aware of this effect when he wrote that "The dissertation 'seduces,' 'animates,' 'misleads,' 'electrifies,' 'inflames'."[21] This theoretical discourse is later meant to be copied in practice.

By taking us back to the most archaic collective structures, Sade's text—much like Laclos's—unveils the most inordinate aspects of collective competition. The time has come for the title of Laclos's novel to be anthropologized: liaisons *are* by nature dangerous; violent reciprocity is everywhere. The war that breaks out between Valmont and Merteuil ends up affecting the whole community. The rivalrous crisis that they seemed to think involved no one but themselves in fact invades others; mimetic interferences begin to saturate all relations.

Baudrillard refuses to consider the mimetic aspects of seduction. For him, the seducer is always already seduced, by his own image, by the illusion that occupies and bewitches him at the same time. The subject is molded less in the image of the other than in the illusion that possesses and propels him. "To seduce is to die as reality and reconstitute oneself as illusion."[22] When Baudrillard takes the other into account, he or she exists only as a power to be ravished. For Baudrillard, this rape is the essence of the seductive strategy: "It is always the story of a murder, or better of an aesthetic and sacrificial immolation."[23]

In contrast to Baudrillard, I would say, rather, that a sort of *mimesis of fear* takes place in seduction. The reversibility of seduction, the aestheticization or spiritualization that Baudrillard seeks as the ultimate step in seduction, takes place only in the camouflaged glow of imitation. Seduction tries to operate as a sort of exorcism of fear. But to do this, it ends up rivalling (imitating) the seducer's own terror of fascination. The same Baudrillard writes apropos of Kierkegaard's *Seducer's Diary* that "The intrigue whereby Cordelia is slowly dispossessed of her powers, makes one think of the innumerable rites for the exorcism of female powers. . . . To cast out women's power . . . to encircle and circumscribe that power, and eventually *simulate* and appropriate it."[24]

Seduction thus takes on all the colors of imitation: camouflage, hypocritical mimicry of the other, unconscious mimetic strategies; but above all else, it assumes certain exacerbated aspects of mediation: hypnosis, possession, poisoning. In all these cases, the person who is seduced is afraid of being inhabited by the other, of being stunned into passivity as the parasitic seducer's host. Metaphors of absorption reveal the refraction of desires in the partners in seduction. This imaginary incorporation of the other into the self is invasive, even fatal. It can lead to death, which is at once deliverance, exorcism, and out-fascination. Death is the outcome of desire exhausted, the outermost limit of confrontation with the other-obstacle. Such is the madness of seduction.

I begin my study with the subtler aspects of imitation—mainly those that masquerade as narcissism—and proceed toward its more elaborate forms (in Laclos, Sade, and Goethe), where imitation is no longer strategic. Here it joins the most sophisticated forms of desire. Mimetic desire is revealed as a satanic knowledge in possession of the other, hallucinatory effects, the desire to be the other's god. *Homo homini deus*: such is the Luciferian vow of seduction.

It is hardly a coincidence that Cazotte wrote his *Diable amoureux* (*The Devil in Love*) near the end of the century (as if in tandem with Charles de Villiers's *Magnétiseur amoureux*).[25] The seducer in this case is the Devil himself. We hear his enchanting voice, his staggering *che vuoi* (the Devil asks *the* essential question of desire); we witness his metamorphoses. He penetrates, hypnotically, the dream of his initiate.

The eighteenth century was quick to proclaim itself the Age of Enlightenment. However, when confronted with desire, this dawning of enlightened Reason saw nothing but the deep, dark night. The day may obstinately push away the night, but night irremediably returns.

Part 1

Sorceresses

Of Coquetry

Marivaux, *The Virtuous Orphan, or the Life of Marianne, Countess of* ***

Marivaux's Marianne makes a veritable philosophy out of coquetry.[1] Indeed, it is a complicated semiology that demands subtle calculations concerning people's intentions. Just how does coquetry operate? The internal property that governs it is vanity. In Marianne, woman is presented as a creature of two minds or spirits: first, a natural one (the seat of reason) and, second, a supplementary property, which is coquetry: "the spirit that the vanity of pleasing gives us" (M, 59). The ratio of nature to culture is difficult to distinguish when it comes to coquetry. This faculty is not assisted by education, from which coquetry learns only its outward form—an air of grace and ease. It would seem that, deep down, coquetry is always already knowledgeable. Over time it gains what the natural spirit can never acquire. Always well-versed, coquetry is lodged in the deepest recesses of the woman; it is somehow consubstantially and generically female.[2] Yet, in Marivaux, coquetry appears as the product of an exchange. It is an imaginary response, a concession to male fantasy: "with an extreme desire to conform to their tastes, we possess the key to everything they do to become ours" (M, 60). More specifically, coquetry is a ruse that women use to combat men's phallic power. It is their only means of responding to the indifference of the other sex, to their arrogant blustering, to their blind self-sufficiency. In *Le Cabinet du philosophe*, Marivaux exposes coquetry as play-acting, as a masquerade with its source in the battle of the sexes. Marivaux, like Joan Riviere much later, defines seduction as a transformation of aggression: as Jacques Lacan explains, "It is for what she is not that [woman] seeks to be desired as well as loved."[3] In *Le Cabinet*, Marivaux's rebellious coquette speaks as follows:

> In the miserable state in which you keep us—deprived of authority, of any activity in which to engage ourselves, of all means to make ourselves feared, as we fear you—was it not imperative for us to make up for the wrongs that your tyranny perpetrates against us, through strength of character and industry? . . . Our malice is but the fruit of our dependence upon you. Our coquetry is our only advantage. We have no other hope than to find favor in your eyes . . . we come out of the void, we know no other way to respect you, to cut a figure, to be something, except to affront ourselves by substituting a humiliating industry, and at times, a vice or two, in the place of the good qualities and virtues that we possess, which you make nothing of, and which you keep captive.[4]

Seduction is described as a negative effort of the self to overcome its status as a nonperson, but at the price of a crippling alienation. Coquetry is a mask, an effacement of true feminine qualities that will never have access to representation. If the coquette believes that she escapes political or social tyranny, it is only to annihilate herself in an even more tyrannical lie, an internalized one, which enslaves her to the desire of the other and forces her to disguise, to veil her true self. If she manages to "cut a figure," as Marivaux puts it, this representation takes place only for the other. All cosmetic contrivances ritualize this failure, this defeat of the subject. There is an undeniably funereal component in the guises the woman adopts to give herself to the other.

Luce Irigaray offers an insightful explanation of this seduction imposed as if naturally up women:

> Feminine beauty seems always to be a costume for—possibly for attracting the other into oneself. It is almost never a manifestation of, the appearance of, a phenomenon expressive of

> exteriority . . . we look at ourselves in the mirror to please someone. . . . The mirror is almost always a means of reducing ourselves to a pure exteriority. . . . The mirror signifies the constitution of that Other, synthesized of surfaces, that I will offer as a prize for seduction "in my place."[5]

Marivaux's stance with respect to female seduction situates him between Nietzsche and Freud. In *The Gay Science*, Nietzsche locates the scandal of female seduction in the fact that the woman must blossom while maintaining her modesty, oppressed as she is by an education that denies her any knowledge of Eros.[6] For Freud, in "On Femininity," female seduction is a compensation or indemnity, an ornamentation of what should remain hidden—genital monstrosity: "The effect of penis-envy has a share, further, in the physical vanity of women, since they are bound to value their charms more highly as a late compensation for their original sexual inferiority."[7]

What makes Marianne our first seductress is the sense of the original lack that is attributed to her, specifically in the figure of the orphan. Marianne's only desire is to be desired—which is to say that her inflamed ego desires all desires. Marivaux plays this exacerbated narcissism to the hilt. In the scene in which the heroine is revealed to us for the first time, she is already surrounded by spectators, whom she has attracted through her cries of misery; she is handed over to the charity and pity of those around her. Marivaux dispossesses his infant character. He forces us to listen to the almost hysterical rhythm of her repeated cries:

> Whilst I was crying . . . five or six gentlemen who were riding by posthaste . . . hearing the cries of a child within, stopped . . . to see what had happened to this child who was crying and to give it their assistance. They looked into the coach, saw there another man who had been killed, and the dead woman fallen by the door, and where, by my cries, they judged I was also. (15)

Marianne is given over to narcissism very early on, fetishized as a doll ("a little princess": *Her Majesty the Baby* . . .), offered up to the admiring gaze of the other.[8] Marivaux exposes her to representation, to the theater of flirtation:

> People came to see me from all the neighboring towns, for I was become an object of curiosity, as well as pity. The superstitious were desirous to examine the features of my face and the lines in my little hands, and foolishly imagined they saw there my sad adventures written in legible characters. Everybody took a kind of romantic fancy to me: they thought me pretty and my air engaging; and you can't imagine how much their natural accomplishments were to my advantage, or how noble and delicate it rendered the tenderness which I inspired. They could not have caressed a little unfortunate princess with greater respect, or a more becoming and graceful air. The ladies, especially, interested themselves in my misfortunes, and were continually making me presents of the finest and genteelest dresses, in which they strove to outview each other. (10)

By consigning his heroine to finery at such an early age, Marivaux seems to pledge her to the reparation of her original lack. In the deployment of this strange compulsion, Marianne wraps herself up in the world of fabrics: "I spent all my childhood being educated, during which time I learned how to make countless different varieties of little ladies' outfits, a trade that served me well in later days" (M, 15). It is no surprise that Marianne will appear threatening when she unmasks herself, shedding the phallic adornments that weigh on her and mark her as a creature destined to please the other. She then appears as the "natural" woman rather than the tricked-out coquette.

Marianne in a Tizzy

Marianne's trump card in seduction soon becomes the sublime effect of her body—as far as it is suggested beneath its layers of wrappings and drapings, the costumes and finery that are the stuff of seduction. Marianne's conquests rely on the power of dress, and the scenes of adornment reveal the heroine's discreet narcissism. She does not attempt to hide the joyous tremor she undergoes in front of her mirror. It is a magic moment for her:

> I then began to dress my head, that I might enjoy at once all my ornaments. I could not look upon my growing beauty, which seemed to increase in proportion as I advanced in dressing, without feeling a kind of pleasing palpitation at my heart, whilst my hand trembled at every pin I stuck. (46)

The unmistakable erotic rush of this scene unfolds progressively: there is imaginary anticipation of the effect of the adornments; repeated manipulation of the props in an erotic, almost masturbatory dance of the hand; and finally, a climax, artfully deferred. If dressing provides this sort of erotic satisfaction, there is something else behind it, a whole science ultimately aimed at woman's power over man:

> When she has found what pleases, it is but a very indifferent discovery, for she must find out what is better, in order to carry it on to its last perfection and finishing excellence. And to attain this, she must read the souls of men, that she may prefer what will gain her the most, rather than what will only gain her much: and this is immense! (47)

With an almost satanic flourish, Marianne thus reveals the secrets of the coquette's trade and her tools of seduction. The spectacle of coquetry is always at the other's disposition, it is always dedicated to the other. In her "read[ing] the souls of men" there is something of Pascal—but it has taken a diabolical twist.[9] In a crucial episode in the novel, when Marianne is due to make a spectacular entrance into Parisian society, she is taken into a church. There, we find her in a lucid frenzy of coquetry, performing a virtual striptease staged with meticulous intent. Having anticipated the scene with contentment ("I was in a hurry to go to church to see how much I would be looked upon" [M, 52]), Marianne finds herself an immediate success: "I was scarce seated before I observed the eyes of all the gentlemen fixed upon me" (50). Marianne's display of charms to the audience of gentlemen has a hypnotic effect on the crowd:

> From time to time, to keep their attention riveted, I would regale them with a little discovery of my charms. I would let them learn something new, without however putting myself at any great expense. For example, in the church there were some paintings hung at a certain height. Well! I would lift my gaze up to them, with the pretext of looking at them, because this little labor made my eyes the prettiest in the world. Then I made use of my hair. It was perfectly coiffed, but I wanted it to come undone so that I might show off my bare hand, which was displayed while rearranging the lock, and which necessarily brought with it a round arm, at least half exposed, poised in the attitude I then assumed. (M, 62)

Seduction requires a sort of fetishistic detachment of the object from the whole. The body must be concretized in separate signs, broken off from the ideal totality, in order to provoke desire; the body as a whole must be kept inaccessible. Although Marianne's beauty is superlative ("the prettiest physiognomy in the world" [M, 62–63]), as a totality it remains on the level of abstraction: it produces itself as an impossible representation:

> Add but one more hand . . . and they will no longer be able to resist, you are delightful. . . . That is because a face, no matter how pleasant, is hardly a nudity . . . but a beautiful hand starts to resemble one, and to captivate certain people one may succeed just as well by tempting them as by satisfying them. (M, 63)

The essential power of seduction lies not in the overly direct gesture of pleasing but in the more calculating act of *temptation.* For the coquette to be "persuasive," there must be a concrete offering of the object (display of hands, of hair, any partial piece of nudity). Temptation is the penetration of the other's desire.

The episode involving Marianne's foot, the occasion of her meeting with Valville, is equally revealing of the heroine's manipulations. The scene begins with a colossal "lapsus," a literal "faux pas."[10] Marianne, "distractedly," is knocked down by Valville's carriage; she has just lost sight of him while leaving church. As the story continues, the accident shows every sign of being engineered. Madame Dutour, always alert, is right to wonder: "How was it that your foot slipped?" (M, 126). The exhibition of Marianne's foot is what will clinch the fascination she already exerts over the young man: "I fancied that I had the prettiest feet in the world; that Valville was going to see them; that it would hardly be my fault that he should do so, since necessity would dictate that I would show them to him" (M, 67). The scene that follows has all the innocent charm of juvenile eroticism. Marianne's foot is innocently held out for examination. Valville's hand slides under the surgeon's. As always with Marivaux, the erotic intention of the act is denied; all is unconscious. But the very perversity of the gesture lies in its unconscious character. Marianne and Valville can both deny any complicity in this innocent episode. Marianne: "My fall was to blame" (M, 67). Valville: "'It looks a little inflamed here' . . . touching his finger to it with an innocent air" (M, 69).

Farewell to innocence at this point, and welcome to a newly discovered Marianne, whose seductions are able to conceal the ferocity of her designs. Let us consider, for example, the episode with Monsieur de Climal, her designated guardian. If Climal appears in the novel as the seducer—the hypocritical figure of Tartuffe immediately comes to mind—one cannot help but wonder how virtuous Marianne really is in relation to him, and whether her position as a victim of his charity does not provide the heroine with a few aces up her sleeve. These are the episodes that we should examine with an eye for Marianne's coquetry and the sexual dimension she adds to it. The function of adornments and finery will certainly aid in our analysis.

Monsieur de Climal's seduction is accomplished through a number of gifts that he is eager to give Marianne. His overly assured manner immediately betrays the amorous purpose of Climal's actions toward Marianne. But what interests me on another level is the precise nature of the presents that he gives her. What Monsieur de Climal does with Marianne is to dress up her femininity so that she will correspond to a certain feminine ideal that he imagines.[11] Climal's gifts are less a charitable act than they are an act of reparation for what Woman does not have. Marianne's guardian fetishizes her, with gloves, dresses, cap, and so forth. In order to understand his gesture, we must also consider the orphaned Marianne as a "figure" of what Climal sees as her original castration, her lack, her primary separation. Climal's seductive operation consists in covering her up with phallic substitutes. Removed from her state of nudity, through a fetishistic branding with clothes and accessories, Marianne will no longer be "nonexistent."[12] Marianne allows herself to fall into Climal's trap, even when she sees through to his thinly disguised intentions. She herself admits that "his extravagance was only intended to bribe my affections" (37)—yet she agrees to parade with him through dressmakers' and milliners' shops. Climal leads Marianne into the unbridled consumption of superfluous objects, directing the girl's first erotic drives to the sumptuous purchases with which, and to which, he seduces her:

> Mr. de Climal had spoken of a suit of clothes which he intended to give me, and we went together to buy it, that I might please my fancy. . . . The clothes were bought. I chose them genteel and modest, and suitable to a young lady not very rich. After this was done, Mr. de Climal talked of linen (and, really, I needed some) and it was immediately purchased. (37)

Even when she refuses his advances, Marianne still insists on keeping all the objects that accentuate her beauty and excite her vanity. She comes up with all sorts of excuses: "I [needed] clothes, and he bought them for me; besides they were grand and genteel, and in my imagination I had already tried them on and found they fitted me exactly" (38). This is what makes the scene in which she returns the gifts to her benefactor so pitiful for the young coquette, who suffers a fell blow to her narcissism. Marianne may very well decide to "pay back" Monsieur de Climal for his charity and to give back everything she had received from him, but she settles the score through a seductive exhibition. Her vanity prompting her to retain all the items that flattered her nascent femininity, she therefore starts out with the objects she is least attached to: "You shall have them all again. And first, I begin with your money, which I have happily about me. . . . Now there only remains the clothes and linen, which I shall presently bundle up for you to take with you in your coach" (92). And then Marianne begins to undress, quite aware of the erotic effect that her performance is having upon Climal. Everything Marianne intends to deny her benefactor, she exhibits in this scene, one might say, in a cruel gesture of provocation:

> whilst I was talking . . . I was unpinning my clothes, and had presently pulled off my cap, because I no longer looked upon it as mine, so that in a moment I stood bareheaded before him, with that beautiful hair that I told you about, that fell all the way down to my waist. This sight entirely disconcerted him. I was in a wild transport, regardless of everything. I raised my voice, and there was nothing to be seen but disorder and confusion and a wild indecorum which alarmed him, and which he seemed to apprehend was in danger of degenerating into an insult upon him. (92)

In this erotic outburst, Marianne—disheveled and dizzily inflamed—takes on for Monsieur de Climal the terrifying face of the Medusa.[13] This metamorphosis of beauty unfolds in an uproar that astonishes the reader and takes Marianne herself by surprise. The text leaves to our imagination the exchange—verging on rape—that follows this disconcerting provocation. Madame Dutour appears to arrive in time. In any case, during this violent altercation, it is difficult to distinguish between the two furious parties:

> I insisted upon going into my room to pack up my clothes. He held me fast, and would not let me go on account of my passion. His lips, pale and trembling, began to open, but what he said I could not perfectly hear. . . . "But, Marianne, are you mad? Why all this noise? Hush, how foolish you make yourself. Come, be quiet. Take care." (92)

Marianne does finally leave to bundle up her clothes. The scene in question reveals the narcissistic wound caused by the idea of giving up her finery:

> In the meantime the bundle was making, and what will doubtless make you smile was that, in the midst of these lofty and couragous thoughts, I could not help considering the linen I was handling, and saying to myself (but so low, that I could scarce hear it), "It is, however, well chosen. How white and fine it is. It is almost a pity to lose it." (98)

And then Marianne's forgetfulness has a role to play:

> There was now my cap to put up. And as I entered the room, I had laid it in a chair near the door, but had quite forgot what I had done with it. A girl of my age, who is going to lose all her finery, may surely be allowed some little absence of mind on so important an occasion. (99)

Marianne will decide to put this cap back on (and she will find all sorts of reasons to justify her action)[14] and the dress Monsieur de Climal had given her as well, when she later goes to visit the monk. She will make use of her finery in order to accuse her "benefactor" of evil designs: "it will be an additional proof" (100); but at the same time she will be able to flatter her vanity one last time: "the only courage I lacked was in regard to the dress" (M, 132). The loss of her clothing and adornments represents a fundamental wound. Marianne cries over her lost objects: "perhaps I was crying for no other reason than my old clothes" (M, 132).

Marivaux insists on exposing all of his heroine's coquettish designs in this cruel scene. He has her hesitate between giving back and keeping the objects of her vanity. Marianne's behavior and techniques are depicted essentially as those of Woman in general: She shows both interest and indifference; playing on all her possibilities, she *oscillates.*

Backstage at the Opera

Marivaux's women always carry mirrors with them. Their coquetry is devoted from the start to the specular doubling of self-seduction, in what is essentially a "composition of vanity."[15] This inner delirium is necessary for the coquette to convince herself that she is capable of seducing others. She must imagine herself as seductive. But the shadow of the other always lurks in the mirror. The other, like reality, can break through into the coquette's imaginary narcissism:

> I saw the belle from afar, as she looked at herself in a mirror, and I noticed, to my great astonishment, that she was admiring herself miming all the expressions that I had seen on her face during our conversation. . . . She caught sight of me in her mirror and blushed. I have just glimpsed, I told her, the backstage machinery at the Opera.[16]

If Marivaux's coquette can exist only in a combative, imaginary relation with men, she also has a need to exist in relation to other coquettes. It could even be claimed that she cares less about attracting male attention than she does about convincing men of her superiority to her companions. Female seduction thus has two aspects: it constitutes the woman as an object of male pleasure but also as an object of female envy.[17] Rivalry thus appears not only as the dynamic element in coquetry but as its playful dimension as well:

> Coquettes do not like each other, and yet they are never happy unless they are together. Do you know what they are seeking in each other's companionship? The pleasure of triumphing

> over each other: they gather to provide nourishment for their vanity, and to rival each other in charm; they contend in face, size, complexion, and in the airs they give themselves.[18]

Rivalrous behavior is necessarily a mimetic conflict: characters confront each other, but their desire for difference is effaced unconsciously by their mutual imitation of gestures and behavior. The only points scored in this futile contest are empty ones. Even beauty itself, which ought to distinguish the coquettes from one another, becomes secondary in this fight for distinction. Victory goes to whoever winks most prettily or whoever knows how to modulate her voice at just the right moment. Marivaux asks the vying twins of coquetry: "Is this a contest of effrontery or beauty?"[19] In Marivaux the coquette is a noisy creature: he speaks of the "fracas of coquetry" that accompanies her and that in some way constitutes the apparatus of her femininity.[20]

In *The Virtuous Orphan,* this kind of rivalry is visible in the church scene we have discussed. Marianne's gaze quickly leaves that of the gentlemen to turn instead toward the women:

> And I was scarce seated before I observed the eyes of all the gentlemen fixed upon me, for I seemed to engage their whole attention; but this was not all. The ladies soon . . . fixed upon me for their rival, who had taken from them the regards of their admirers. (50)

Marianne wishes to distinguish herself from the other coquettes. The fact that she recognizes spite, anger, and envy in the coquette's eyes shows to what extent she is familiar with these sentiments herself. And it must be said that what these coquettes reflect back to her is only the projected image of male desire. These women, Marianne tells us, "were in extremely fancy dress" (M, 88). They are themselves pure exteriority, phallicized to the extreme. Above all, Marianne sees them as models of seduction: straightaway they become rivals, competitors to be outdone, obstacles to be eliminated.

Marianne's seductive posture reveals her mild erotomania,

that is, the blindly persistent belief that she constitutes the other's object of desire. Defining feminine erotomania, Piera Aulagnier-Spairani writes that the affected woman "is sure that she possesses the object that will never be overlooked by a man's gaze or, better, by the gaze of desire."[21] For Marianne to occupy the locus of attention, to be at the center of all gazes, she need only be present.

René Girard was right to see the coquette's self-sufficiency as a ruse of desire: she feigns detachment and self-absorption the better to attract the attentive gaze of others. In fact the coquette needs others' desire in order to be sure of her own desire. Her desire for herself is even the exacerbated form, the distillation of the desires exercised on her by others. It is the ultimate impregnation of these desires. It is necessary in this case to adopt a new statement on narcissism: you can't love if you don't love yourself first—you can't seduce if you don't seduce yourself first. And it is difficult to understand why Sarah Kofman so violently rejects Girard's analysis. Kofman effectively uses Freud against Girard: In Freud, she maintains, women retain their narcissism while men lose it entirely in their eternal search for the love object; men can love only through a transfer (delegation) of their original narcissism. However, Freud himself comes under Kofman's attack for another faux pas when, after his brilliant correction to his article on femininity, he characterizes pregnancy as an abandonment of female narcissism, as the woman's inevitable accession to objectal love. Without expatiating on the debate that opposes both Girard and Kofman to Freud's text on narcissism, I might point out that Kofman crudely truncates Girard's thought for the benefit of her own argument.[22] Women, in Girard's analysis, are indeed denied the privilege of self-sufficiency—but so are men. Girard's mimetic scenario is more flexible than Kofman claims. Human beings are constantly changing roles in the mimetic whirlwind, which has them falling into their own traps; the woman "*has no more self-sufficiency than the man who desires her*," writes Girard.[23]

In his analysis of Freud's text, Mikkel Borch-Jacobsen goes a long way toward clarifying this claim of female self-sufficiency. He reminds us first of what Freud wrote: "Strictly speaking, it is only themselves that such women love with an intensity *comparable to that of the man's love for them*" (emphasis added). Borch-Jacobsen supports Girard's position by "deconstructing" the narcissism Freud at first ascribed to woman. He concludes: "she loves as man does. More precisely, she loves like the man who loves a woman who loves as a man does—in order to be loved. . . . There is no narcissism but the narcissism of the other. It takes two (at least) to make a Narcissus."[24]

To fall into the trap of female self-sufficiency is to place the woman, precisely, in a sort of no-man's land, where she can be deified as a separate, nonrelational creature. (True, Kofman prefers the castrating figures of the criminal, the animal of prey, evoked by Freud.) Marivaux does not fall into this trap. But his narcissistic coquette maintains a relation of denial vis-à-vis her love object. The coquette, he tells us, does not know how to love; she knows only how to please.[25] The posture of pleasing ultimately excludes a relation with the other. It creates between self and other the distance of the *spectacle*.

The Crying Game

Marianne reveals other means of seduction to us. Tears are her most immediate trump card, her most liquid asset. Her tears pour out in front of others like a kind of virtuous secretion, innocent and pure. But in point of fact, the conditioning that precedes the tears is often quite striking. For example, when she cries to convince the monk of Monsieur de Climal's seduction, the description of her advance preparation proposes a whole physiology of tears:

> I collected matter for my grief from almost every object that presented itself. My soul instructed itself in everything that could heighten and aggravate my misfortunes; and this was not a time for tears. We only set open the sluices of grief, when our sorrows are risen to a proper height and swell too high to be confined within their banks. (101)

Marianne shows her consummate art of lamentation when she stands before Madame de Miran, the benefactress who definitively replaces Climal. Marianne knows how to offer her body in affliction. The posture she assumes is the very image of grief. If she feigns self-forgetfulness in the absorption of her pose, it is the better to capture the other's gaze; her charming attire only intensifies the effect.

> my moving complaints reached her ears. . . . I was seated, with bowed head, while my arms hung lifelessly, and I was so swallowed up with my calamities that I even forgot where I was. My affliction, which appeared to her the most extreme, sensibly touched her . . . and perhaps, too, my dress, contributed to interest her in my grief; if I mention my dress, it is because it certainly didn't hurt my cause. (111; M, 146)[26]

The encounter with Madame de Miran can be viewed as a veritable amorous seduction. All the signs of love at first sight—blushing, eye contact—are present:

> At the noise she made in retiring, I came to myself. And, as I heard somebody's steps, I was willing to see who it was; she expected it, and our eyes instantly met. I could not see her without blushing at being surprised in my lamentations. But in spite of all my confusion, I observed she was pleased with my looks, and that my affliction touched her. (111)

In the economy of the novel, the accidental meeting with Valville that we have discussed finds another meaning: it leads Marianne, the orphan, directly to this adoptive mother. She is able to love the mother through her son:

> "I at first sight conceived an inclination for him without knowing it was love. I did not think myself in danger of feeling that passion. . . . He is a young man of such a graceful appearance, so perfectly agreeable, and so like you, Madam, for you know I loved you at first sight: *my passions for you are exactly the same*." (143; emphasis added)

When Valville later becomes unfaithful to Marianne, it is understandable why, in spite of her jealousy, she recovers so rapidly from that loss. Valville's departure works to Marianne's advantage, by allowing her to have Madame de Miran all to herself. And the mother will go so far as to deny the son in order to adopt the daughter, removing the last obstacle to Marianne's amorous attachment to Madame de Miran. Seduction is here preceded by a separation: in order to realize her desire, Marianne does everything she can to sever the bonds between mother and son. She occupies the space of filiation by feigning the greatest devotion. Her desire is inscribed in the text through an anagram: Miran/Marianne form a complementary pair in the mirrored resemblance of their names. The girl experiences the imagined loss of Madame de Miran (provoked by Valville's unfaithfulness) as a loss of maternal space, of maternity as a locus, as an enclosure, a fold of gentleness and tenderness: "I not only thought that Valville was unfaithful, but that his mother would no longer be mine, and that I should never possess that apartment she had shown me at her house, which was so near to hers" (287).

Marianne's seduction of Madame de Miran turns out to be successful. The first of the various stages presented by the text is Marianne's vow: " 'You know, my dear mother, I love Mr. de Valville, but still my heart is more yours than his. My gratitude to you is dearer to me than my love' " (209). Valville's withdrawal—" 'I have not a heart so noble as yours yet that of my mother is as worthy as yours' " (M, 288)—is followed by Madame de Miran's definitive verdict: " 'She is worth more than you'." All that remains is to remake Marianne's birth, to efface the biological beneath the spiritual. Madame de Miran announces this "symbolic" pregnancy when she instructs Marianne to "think that thou shalt forever be my daughter, and thou possessest the first place in my heart" (308). The desired link having been obtained, Marianne can once again display her charms, her triumphant coquetry: "I cried less from chagrin, I think, than from a desire to appear adorable" (M, 144).

I would go so far as to say that the "symbolic" mother functions as the mediator of Marianne's desire (for aristocracy, for wealth, for filiation). Let us not forget that Miran is the model of maternity dreamt of by Marianne.[27] The megalomaniacal mediation that Madame de Miran makes possible for Marianne is based on the principle of the soul, this transcendent entity, this Other that she invents, of which she believes she is the living example, and against which all other beings can be compared and classified. Blood relations can be deceiving; they are a false criterion, as certain appearances can threaten them. Only the soul (or the heart) can be relied on to hierarchize relations truthfully within the community.

Thus Marivaux pairs two types of seduction in this novel, thereby granting Marianne a particularly complex *Bildung*. One phase comprises two aspects, one of which could initially be identified as castrating. Marianne must embody an image that has been dreamed up for her, corresponding to the fetishistic desire of others. She is placed under the tyranny of their gaze. Marianne's femininity is represented as a lack to be filled, a narcissism consisting entirely in negation (dissatisfaction, sense of inferiority, sexual passivity). The realization of femininity must take place through the appropriation of an imaginary ideal model, a stereotyped *sex object*: Marianne must become beautiful, she must master the art of being attractive. The second aspect of this same phase is the rivalry it implies with other women. The models of coquetry multiply before the girl's astonished eyes. She will corner the masculine market only by crushing her rivals. Marianne's narcissism appears not only as an extravagant ego, a mechanism of manic self-sufficiency, but also as a series of copied mannerisms, imitations of seductive poses. Marianne may believe her coquetry is exceptional, but her seduction does not escape the most banal, coded, formulaic instruction. It is a cookie-cutter, carbon-copy, flim-flam seduction—but one that basks in the illusion of escaping such assembly-line mass production. Marianne's exhibitionism, her display of finery, and the whole erotic and fetishistic grammar that she deploys are not in her case—so she believes—the repetition of familiar feminine affectations. They are in some sense, because of the beauty of the body that displays them, *original*. Marianne makes her own flirtation the standard; she absolutizes her seduction.

Marivaux has his heroine experience a second phase of seduction, however. She is freed from her imaginary imprisonment and given over to a new type of individuation. The space of rivalry with other women gives way to feminine understanding. The first part of the novel is corrected by the second, the latter being written under the sign of continuity with the mother. The burdensome gallery of rival-models is replaced in this second half by a transcendent model, one that cannot be attained by negative, destructive competition. Madame de Miran's mediation leads Marianne to achieve a femininity that falls under the aegis of benevolence, affection, interiority, and understanding. Marianne's intelligence is no longer simply a "jewel of great beauty" (M, 21) added to her panoply of ornaments, no longer just another feather in her coquettish cap, an admission ticket to the theater of seduction; rather, in Marianne's connectedness to Madame de Miran, the heroine's intelligence is proof of meditative activity. A far cry from artifice, this intelligence is close to being itself.

Poison

Prévost, *Manon Lescaut*

en blancheur sybilline la femme . . .
—MALLARMÉ

Manon is an apparition. But at the beginning of Prévost's text, she is also the picture of defilement.[1] The novel's aesthetic development notwithstanding, the backdrop against which the author places Manon harbors a hideous spectacle. A mob looks on. The curiosity, commotion, and confusion smack of some horrible ritual. We see women being thrust in front of others, a prey to their gaze: creatures of the night are suddenly exposed to the blinding light of day. The spectacle is heightened by the imposing police machinery, a corps of musket-carrying soldiers, watched over by the lieutenant-general of police. A single pair of eyes in the crowd, an old woman, cries out against the barbarity. The disorder, tumult, and strangeness of the ritual lend the scene the appearance of a collective lynching. The wagons of chained prostitutes bring to mind the ships of fools that carried those otherworldly beings far from the shores of Reason. This crossing is the last leg of the journey. The name Manon is the one that will endure for these vestal priestesses of Pleasure.

The Goncourt brothers later attempted to save Prévost's heroine by distancing her from the lugubrious courtesan stories of the period. Manon escapes the libertine label by being poeticized: "the moment one touches this story of prostitutes past, one sees delicately rising from the ashes of vice, from this fine dust of scandal—like an exquisite scent emanating from putrescence—this heroine of a deathless novel."[2] But in so rescuing Manon, the Goncourts render the spectacle of her embarkation banal. The real eighteenth century was less demure. But the Goncourt brothers themselves were blind to the ambivalence of the spectacle they describe as an innocent carnival—as if to deny that the laughter and the festive ribbons hide the same victimary rite beneath the innocuous appearance of a festival:

> We see hundreds of couples coming down from the Church of the Priory of Saint-Martin des Champs—the line of wagons filled with vulgar gaiety, the troop of prostitutes, all those laughing faces . . . amongst thousands of ribbons and bright yellow bands: what noise! what splendor! A passer-by's name is called out from a wagon; an abbott is jeered by a chorus of voices. Not a whit of remorse, not a whit of concern in all these creatures: how far removed they are from the musing melancholic posture that Abbé Prévost's imagination lends the defeated and despairing body of his heroine set upon the straw as the wagon sets off for Le Havre! They parade along, preceded by their men who wear their colors, the bright yellow rosettes on their hats. . . . One last mercy is granted them in this carnival, this nuptial masquerade that makes their heads spin as they are sent off into exile.[3]

The "Oh, it's nothing" (25) of the archer, explaining the commotion of the prostitutes' departure to the man of quality, would fit perfectly into the tableau described by the Goncourt brothers: it is a joyous celebration. But Prévost decided to add a discordant note: an old lady's cry of pity and the gentleman's look of compassion.

The figure of Manon that appears in this inaugural scene is contradictory. She is both defiled and divine. The modesty of her expression deflects any suspicion of profligacy. Manon seems to efface herself as a sexual object. Her immediate seductiveness lies in this pose of absorption, a turning inward on herself that seems oblivious to the observing crowd:

> She was in abject misery and her clothes were filthy, but all that had so little effect on her beauty that I felt nothing but pity and respect for her. She was trying to turn away as much as the chains would allow, so as to hide her face from us onlookers, and this effort at concealment was so natural that it seemed to come from feelings of modesty. (26)

Manon is thus presented straightaway as a *fascinum*, a Medusa whose mysterious charm transfixes.[4] To come near her is to be touched by the feminine enigma: "she sounded so charming and modest that I found myself making many a reflection on the inscrutable nature of woman," the man of quality concludes (29).

If Marianne preserves her virtue while managing to hold on to Monsieur de Climal's gifts—and thus escapes any awareness of being fetishized by money—by contrast Manon, from the beginning, is presented as participating in illicit exchanges. We can already tally up the sum: four louis d'or, two louis, six louis d'or from the man of quality. For the privilege of being near her, Des Grieux has already surrendered his money and his horse. Such is the commerce to which Prévost's heroine is reduced as her destiny is put on the block: "every time I have had permission to speak to her I have had to pay" (27). Manon is subjected to the brutal law of economic transactions between men; even her lover is forced to participate in this humiliating trade. The novel encodes Manon's character perfectly from the start: defilement, divinity, commodity. The narrative will unfold this triple metamorphosis in parallel.

Manon, I submit, constitutes the first step in the degeneration of the coquette.[5] Manon occupies the locus of an exchange that is no longer ludic but mercantile. Eroticism is no longer playful; rather, it is purely a mechanism of economic repetition. The joyous narcissistic enticement of Marivaux's coquettes is completely absent here. Pleasure is governed no longer by the law of desire but by the laws of the marketplace. If Manon glitters like gold, if her destiny is reflected in the lustrous gleam of a few louis, the text leaves this exchange in the realm of the enigmatic. A sort of compulsion drives Manon toward prostitution. The event in question always comes as a surprise—but an inevitable one. The reader is left bemused, like her lover Des Grieux.

Manon circulates in a sort of ethereal, enigmatic atmosphere. The mystery is immediately perceived as the enigma of her entire sex. The man of quality has just given six louis d'or to ensure that Des Grieux will be able to continue seeing Manon; immediately, he himself goes to exchange a few words with his new friend's mistress. He returns, struck by the "inscrutable nature of woman" (29). Luce Irigaray's remarks are helpful in understanding Manon's particular situation:

> woman thus has value only in that she can be exchanged. . . . Women-as-commodities are thus subject to a schism that divides them into the categories of usefulness and exchange-value; into matter-body and an envelope that is precious but impenetrable, ungraspable, and not susceptible to appropriation by women themselves; into private use and social use.[6]

Women can therefore exist as commodities, but beyond that they remain out of reach. Manon's enigma becomes even more apparent when we analyze Des Grieux's situation. Although he is a total stranger to the man of quality, Des Grieux's social position is transparent, his distinction natural, self-evident: "a mere glance is all you need to gauge a man's birth and upbringing. As I went over to him he stood up, and I could see in his eyes, face and every movement such gentle refinement that I instinctively felt kindly disposed towards him" (26–27). Despite the generosity of the man of quality and the effect Manon's suffering has on him, it is through Des Grieux, by means of a sort of essentialized aristocratic seduction that the latter effects upon him (through his reveries, tears, handsome features, grace, and gentility), that the man of quality is eager to offer his services.

In the Shadow of Tiberge

The scope of Manon's seduction is impossible to understand without studying Des Grieux's role in the narrative. If the two characters are subsequently presented as reflections of one another—"He must be her brother, or else a lover" (26)—their sexual motivations will make of them entirely separate beings. These differences appear right from the moment of their first meeting. Des Grieux presents Manon thus:

> The way I spoke to her soon made her realize the state of my feelings, for she was much more experienced than I was. I gathered that she was being sent to the convent against her will, and I see now that it was probably to check the pleasure-loving tendencies that had already shown themselves in her. (32–33)

In contrast, Des Grieux himself is characterized by a certain chasteness: "I am quiet and gentle by disposition and studious by nature. Moreover a certain instinctive aversion from evil was credited to me as a positive virtue" (31). Consequently, this initial meeting is a shock for Des Grieux. All his senses are revealed to him for the first time: "I had not been in love for more than a minute, but already love had so sharpened my wits that in a flash I made up my mind" (32); Manon's appearance strikes him with self-knowledge. It is easy to understand why this encounter is depicted as so fateful. We witness a sort of abortive action that upsets everything, annuls his narcissistic contemplation, and introduces guilt into his infantile territory once and for all: "how I wish I had fixed [my leaving for Amiens] a day earlier!" (32).

We must read this crucial encounter in the context of Des Grieux's virtuous ideality (he tells us that he was "an example" at school, the idol of all the town [31]), of a challenge to narcissistic, infantile closure; but above all of the homoerotic friendship between Des Grieux and Tiberge, with whom he is linked, he confides, through ties of friendship "surpassing the most famous examples in antiquity" (31).[7] If Des Grieux aspires to a certain *aphanisis*, that is, to an invincible containment of the senses if not a disappearance of sexual desire, it is because of Tiberge. Despite the passionate outbursts between them, their relationship is based strictly on prudence and sensual restraint, in essence a refusal of the opposite sex—a refusal that makes any spilling over of eroticism between them all the more dangerous. Des Grieux's shyness is clearly expressed along these lines: "My modesty and reserve had been the admiration of all who knew me, and I had never so much as given a thought to the difference between the sexes, or more than a passing glance to any woman" (32). Tiberge exhibits a timid jealousy after the first encounter between Des Grieux and Manon. He sets the privileged status of their friendship over against his friend's choice: "I ended by taking him into my confidence about the whole affair. He heard me with such obvious disapproval that I trembled. . . . He said that he was too intimate a friend of mine not to oppose the idea with all his might" (35). Later, when Des Grieux undergoes his first imprisonment, even he is surprised by the emotional outpourings of his best friend. Although dismayed, he excuses the erotic tone of his friend's sentiments:

> One day Tiberge came to see me in my prison. The warmth of his affection quite took me by surprise, for so far I had not had any proofs of his feelings towards me which justified my thinking of them as anything more than the usual college friendship which springs up between young fellows of about the same age. (48)

Tiberge's rivalry vis-à-vis Manon is expressed in the symmetrical way Des Grieux and he find solitude to be wanting with the absence of the love object and the suppression of the ego. Des Grieux: "to make this peaceful retirement delightful beyond all possibility of improvement, Manon would have to be there" (50). Tiberge: "Can you guess . . . what has prevented me from seeking the peace of the solitary life? Simply my friendship for you" (49).

Des Grieux is one of the rare antiseductive characters in the eighteenth-century novel. Not only does he reject libertinage, but moreover he squelches desire—both homo- and heteroerotic. Tiberge condemns his friend's attachment to the frivolous Manon. He proposes replacing the poison of seduction with *virtue*, an asexual diet, a transcendence of pleasures in a fantasized reality: "The lust of the flesh has led you astray, and what a loss it has been for the forces of good!" (49).

Des Grieux is caught in the dilemma of having two objects from which to choose: one within a homosocial morality, which implies a rejection of sexuality and women; the other (which is however a consequence of the first) in the figure of the whore. Des Grieux is condemned to these two extremes. What Freud calls "love for a harlot" in his *Sexuality and the Psychology of Love* develops similarly for Prévost's characters. Asceticism (which keeps all libidinal temptation at a distance) and love for a prostitute stem from the same root: an original abasement of the sexual object. Freud's description of the way jealousy functions for such people is familiar: "Not until they have some occasion for jealousy does their passion reach its height and the woman acquire her full value to them, and they never fail to seize upon some incident by which this intensity of feeling may thus be called out."[8]

This is borne out by Des Grieux, who finding himself utterly unoccupied has no other aim but to witness his mistress's debauchery (his period of activity at the Hôtel de Transylvanie is a short one; he counts endlessly on inheriting his family fortune). Manon is drawn inexorably back into libertinage by a kind of fatality (the motivation for which could be located in the unconscious): her lover's lack of wealth, repeated incidents such as fires, thefts, and so on. The more Manon betrays him, the more faithful Des Grieux becomes. Faced with his mistress's wild expenditures, he displays at all times an impassive constancy. *Constancy becomes his neurosis.* When Manon sends him a courtesan, he at first feigns infidelity, trying to desire it, but he rapidly returns to his previous sentiments for Manon, not finding in the courtesan "those soft and lovely eyes, that godlike carriage, that complexion mixed in Love's own palette—in a word the inexhaustible wealth of charms which Nature had lavished on my faithless Manon" (131). But what stands out most in this scene is the sexual abasement that explains Des Grieux's sentimental posture and also, doubtless, his fright vis-à-vis the sex that seems so unfamiliar, so *other* to him:

> "Come here, my child," I said to the girl, "Come here, since you have been sent to console me" . . . [S]he came and tried to give me a few caresses. I immediately thrust her aside, however. "What do you expect from me?" I said, "you are a woman, you belong to a sex which I abominate and have finished with for good." (133)

Des Grieux's constancy has something of the ascetic about it; it is the glorious badge of his first infantile fixations. He displays it in place of that which he does not possess—the phallic object: "As for me, I have nothing to offer but love and constancy. Women scorn my poverty and use my simplicity for their sport" (133). Unlike the seducer in other novels, the plaything that Des Grieux has become in *Manon* will never be, precisely, the phallic object that women seeking to amuse themselves pass one another with a kind of playful levity; rather, he is designated as a refusal of pleasure. Des Grieux, the victim of his own constancy, becomes the object of the castrating libertine irony of women. Wealth, houses, carriages, all those "seductive goods" that he accuses others of having, are but the alibi he fixes on to excuse his impotence.

Confrontation with other males continually reveals an emasculated Des Grieux:

> "I was seized by three men whom I recognised as my father's lackeys. They did not rough-handle me, but two of them pinioned my arms while the third went through my pockets and removed the only weapon I had on me, a small knife." (41)

> "I leaped for my sword, but, as ill-luck would have it, it was entangled with my belt. . . . They quickly had me defenceless." (147)

After his "mortal jealousy" over Manon's affair with Monsieur de G. M., Des Grieux experiences an unusual phallic awakening. He threatens them with his dagger, but this "outburst" fails, for straightaway Des Grieux collapses: "I dropped into a chair, and my hat fell to the floor on one side and my stick on the other" (132). He discovers his feminine affect, his infantile inner world once again: "tears began to run down my cheeks as my fit of rage turned into abject misery. I was reduced to weeping, groans and sighs" (132). Finally, in the scene in which he digs Manon's grave, he renounces his phallic sword in favor of more loving, infantile hands.

The sole instance of intimacy that Manon accords Des Grieux is used to feminize him. He is fetishized, adorned by the hands of his lover: if he is phallicized, it is as Manon's fetish. In fact, in front of the Prince of Italy Manon treats her lover with a brutality that is hardly meant to flatter him, but that he accepts because this move on the part of his mistress at least shams exclusive possession:

> When I woke up Manon informed me that by spending the day at home she did not mean that she wanted me to look slovenly, and she proposed to dress my hair with her own hands. I had a very fine head of hair and she had often amused herself in this way. But this time she took more care over the task than I had ever known her take before. To satisfy her, I had to sit in front of her dressing-table and submit to every little device she could think of for my embellishment. . . . I was indulgently submitting to her every wish when it was announced that the Prince of *** was asking to see her. This name filled me with fury. "What!" I cried, pushing her away from me, "Who? What prince?" She made no answer. "Show him up," she cooly said to the servant. . . . Hearing the ante-room door open, she grasped my floating hair in one hand, seized her mirror in the other, and exerting all her strength hauled me in that state across the room, pushed the door open with her knee, and presented the stranger . . . with a sight that must have caused him no little astonishment. . . . "Look, Sir. . . . Here is the man I love. . . . All

the princes in Italy are not worth one of the hairs I am holding in my hand." (119–20)

Manon's Moods

Des Grieux's unconscious desire for Manon's infidelity is the ultimate mimetic strategy. If Des Grieux accepts Manon's prostitution, it is in order to be able to desire her. Freud is right to describe the situation of the prostitute's lover as that of an "injured third party."[9] What this amusing phrase expresses is the bizarre side of mediation. Des Grieux's desire has value only through interest that others show in his mistress: "It was no crime on Manon's part that people fell in love with her" (117). "I was most gratified by the power of her charms and congratulated myself on being loved by a woman whom everybody found so lovable" (123). Manon's promiscuity should be seen as the projection of Des Grieux's erotic desire, which requires this kind of abjection, the debasement of the object. Des Grieux turns Manon into a real sex object, at once violently desired and scorned. Naturally, he pretends that he is a stranger to jealousy and finds all sorts of reasons for justifying its absence: "I did not have any feeling of jealousy. . . . That lovely creature was so completely mistress of my heart that I harboured no emotions other than respect and love" (123).

This mimetic strategy betrays the desperate emptiness of the desiring subject. How can we not pity Des Grieux's cries of inner turmoil: "Have I anything worthy to be weighed in the balance against her? . . . For me she is glory, happiness and fortune" (110). The perversion to which this mimetic strategy will lead includes Des Grieux's willingness to participate in libertine games, to take his place—in his imagination—behind Manon's seducers. Monsieur de T. communicates to him this "most amusing idea": "it seemed to him that the most enjoyable way I could take revenge on my rival would be to eat his supper and spend the night in the bed he was hoping to share with my mistress" (144). Unfortunately, the ending of the story robs Des Grieux of this pleasurable moment of vengeance: Monsieur de G. M. "arrived just as I was getting into bed" (147).

In New Orleans, where the lovers retreat far from libertine circles, Manon's faithfulness is threatened once again. The marriage code of the colony bestows Manon on the governor's nephew. Even in death, it could be said, she is destined to pass into yet another man's hands. The last man to want to share her, Synnelet, has her body transported elsewhere, thus undoing the grave that Des Grieux had dug with his own hands, in which he had placed "the idol of [his] heart" (188) wrapped in all her apparel.

If Manon represents the zenith of seduction, it is because of the way she manages to interiorize the process: we are never allowed to view her libertinage. She manages to keep the dramatically public side of her morals quite private. The reader (like Des Grieux) is witness only to the aftermath of her seductions: "I learned that [Monsieur de B.] had seen her at the window, desired her passionately . . . that she had given in little by little" (55). The text rarely exhibits the fruits of her coquetry: pearl necklaces, jewels, and money are mentioned only in passing.

Manon's seduction of Des Grieux partakes of the same secrecy[10]; but the effect on him is diabolical. She bewitches him through her charm, her magical presence. Tiberge, who envies the space that Manon occupies in Des Grieux's soul, calls her a poison. According to him, she has done nothing less than cast a spell on his friend, as if with some magic philter—poison or potion, the two words share the same origin, the same effect. Des Grieux himself is the victim of what he accuses Monsieur de B. of having used to seduce his mistress: "he has seduced her by some charm or even drug" (45). Manon is Des Grieux's narcotic: "a kind of ineffable warmth spread through my whole being and I experienced such overpowering emotion that for some time I could not utter a sound" (34). If she resembles him, it is the better to possess him: "I lived in her alone," Des Grieux confides (38). It is easy to understand that she makes Des Grieux "ill": he suffers loss of consciousness, aphasia, shudderings. A pusher of desire, Manon prefigures Sade's pharmacist-seductress, who displays her panoply of philters and aphrodisiacs in broad daylight. As a "Venus" (71), Manon is first and foremost venomous. For Des Grieux she is also "a wonderful alchemist . . . [who] changes everything into gold" (177).

Manon makes her diabolical entrance at Saint-Sulpice where she comes to desecrate Des Grieux's spiritual exercises and to take the place of his object of worship; hence, the profane mixture "of amorous and theological language" (55) that accompanies Des Grieux's initial shock. But this apparition takes place in a fairy-tale atmosphere. Manon is a spell-binder with a diabolical effect on Des Grieux: she provokes terror, trembling, "panic fear" (54). The illness that haunts him after her death is like a languishing continuation of her spell, until the final exorcism: "[God] shed his light upon me" (189).

As much as Des Grieux is characterized by stasis (desire for rest, tranquility, constancy), Manon, waylaid in the course of her first flight from home, in a coach from Amiens, is epitomized by her mobility.[11] Right up to her death, Manon continues to be transported, tossed about from hand to hand, from shore to shore, from tomb to tomb.

Must Des Grieux's choice of object be explained as a filial fixation on pubescent phantasms, by his relation to his mother? We know that his mother is absent from the text and that the voice of the Father lays down the law. But Des Grieux mentions his mother at the end to implore forgiveness for Manon: "Think of my mother," Des Grieux begs his father (164). These phantasms could explain the fact that Manon is courted by Monsieur de G. M., father, and Monsieur de G. M., son, at the same time. The fortuitousness of this incestuous mimetic relationship makes sense when considered from this particular angle of the story.

In any case, Manon's death allows Des Grieux to return to his first tendencies, to his original asceticism. He thus regains the purest form of his desire—the form by which Manon kept him at a distance, by constantly deferring it: castration. Naturally, Tiberge is the person who welcomes his friend back to morality and family responsibility. Tiberge regains the privilege of being the sole Model he so desired to be in his friend's eyes. But what he sees in Des Grieux is an idealized image of himself. At Saint-Sulpice, seduced by the perfection of his "handiwork" (52), he was overjoyed to the point of tears. The final conversion, this return to virtue (that sublimated region of passion that sealed their friendship), fails to conceal the eroticism of their relationship: "I gave him unexpected joy by declaring that the seeds of virtue he had sown long ago in my heart were beginning to bear fruit which he would approve of" (190). Des Grieux will bear Tiberge's child. . . .

Manon in Song

Massenet's opera transports us into the heady atmosphere of finery and adornment—gowns, jewelry, glittering gold—even more emphatically than the novel on which it is based. In the opera, the characters Poussette, Javotte, and Rosette exteriorize coquetry in a way that is absent from Prévost's text, which only furtively mentions Manon's promenades in the Bois de Boulogne with her young female friends and their "little excursions and trivial feminine occupations" (116). In the libretto by Henri Meilhac and Philippe Gille, however, Poussette and company locate Manon in a feminine world: "How pretty are these women! The youngest wore a necklace of gold nuggets. Oh! their sumptuous gowns and darling adornments made them all the more enchanting!" Manon makes her entrance in Act III surrounded by the milliners and other vendors of the Cours la Reine: "Look here! slippers with flowerets. . . . Kerchiefs and hoods; Bonnets, petticoats, and ruffs! . . . Gauze, linens and muffs!" (III, i). In Act IV the same characters are transported to the Hôtel de Transylvanie, where the coquettes show us even more of what lies behind appearances. Their bodily seduction conceals another type of seduction. The coquette dreams less of love than she does of gold: "And for Manon still more gold, more gold, more gold!" (IV, ii). Right through the moment of her collapse (in Act V), Manon glides along deliriously on the wishes (the words) of Des Grieux;

she never sings her salvation (heaven), but only her thirst for adornment (jewels): to Des Grieux's observation, "Night is falling now, the first star has appeared!" Manon replies, "Ah! The lovely diamond! You see, I am still a coquette!" (V, v).

Massenet's librettists made explicit what remained interiorized and private in Prévost's novel. They put the splendor of coquetry back on the market of appearances. The music trips frivolously along through this libertine economy. In the opera Manon dies happily, singing the end of her own story. Massenet also allows the coquette her own narcissism—which in Prévost's novel is always transmitted through Des Grieux. Here, on the contrary, Manon can sing the praises of her own beauty. Her voice is her mirror: "I reign through my beauty" (III, iv).

Manon also regains her mobility in the opera. From the start she confides to her cousin: "Don't laugh when I tell you that I thought I had wings and was flying to paradise" (I, iv). She seems to forge ahead, with pure velocity, racing her own destiny ("Who knows," she says, like an eighteenth-century Célimène, "who knows if we'll be alive tomorrow! . . . Youth disappears, beauty fades away . . . [IV, ii]; "Let us take full advantage of our youth . . . while we are only twenty!" [III, iv]). But she also precipitates toward her consumption, her expenditure, her exhaustion: "My horses gallop apace, racing my daring life" (III, iv). Manon's seduction is caught up in this impossible rhythm that strives to keep ahead of life. For her, life is adventure; to keep moving means to master time and defer death.

The opera's crucial scene of seduction (III, iii) also brings out Manon's diabolical powers of enchantment. At the church when Des Grieux prepares to turn inward in a spiritual exercise, an attempt to replace worldly images with those of God, Manon disturbs his tranquility with a temptation that takes two forms. The first and more terrifying of the two is an image, which prefigures the real seduction in an imaginary, erotic reminder of the body: "Flee, sweet image" (III, tableau 2, iii). Second comes temptation in the intermediary guise of the voice that announces presence: "Listen to me!" And finally,

Manon appears. Her entire body is enlisted in this sensual seduction; yet, this presence remains an imaginary one, experienced as memory, as an intoxicating recollection: "Is it no longer my hand that this hand presses? Is this no longer my voice? . . . Am I no longer myself? . . . Is this no longer Manon?" (III, tableau 2, vii).

Massenet's opera succeeds brilliantly in conveying the specular trap that ensnares the two lovers. But above all, it shows Des Grieux's total absorption in the object of his desire. Des Grieux's promise to wed Manon is accompanied by his wish for her to bear his name: "And my name will become yours!" (I, viii). The final aria, which echoes the one accompanying Manon's return to Des Grieux, once again intermingles the two characters: "Is it no longer my hand that this hand presses? . . . It is his hand that this hand presses" (V, v). The alternation of pronouns and the reversibility of the intertwined subjects efface the duo into a corporeal and vocal echo.

Massenet is ultimately successful in keeping Manon's secret, the sybilline femininity of this sphynx whose heart is "triply feminine" to Des Grieux. But the opera succeeds above all in giving voice to what remained unheard in Prévost's text, what failed to penetrate her silent beauty: that is, the seduction of her bewitching voice. Out of the distance between Des Grieux and Manon, the impossible convergence of their desires, Massenet draws a melodic temptation: "Manon, amazing sphynx, consummate siren" (IV, ii).

Forbidden Liaisons

Diderot, *The Nun*

It is no accident that we first encounter Suzanne in the context of her family. If we discount the separation between the sexual device of the novel (the convents) and the familial setting, we can see that the seductions in the second part of the novel are simply a reprise, in another mode, of what happens in the "domestic" sphere. The crux of the second part of *The Nun* is still Suzanne's particular condition: the fact that she is illegitimate. This is what explains her difference within the nucleus of her family and her desire to resemble her sisters. Suzanne's participation in the family structure is blocked at every turn (marriage is impossible, a dowry is denied her, and so on). The moment Suzanne learns of her illegitimacy, she instantly finds herself an orphan: "I had no father, religious scruples had deprived me of a mother, precautions had been taken against my claiming the rights of legitimate birth" (38).[1]

It could be said that this illegitimacy is less a real condition than a manifestation of Suzanne's desire. The absence of a birth and the ordeal of weaning force her to desire the very thing that has been denied her. This is the artificial situation dramatized at the beginning of Diderot's novel.

Suzanne finds herself caught up in a process of endlessly desiring the mother who has been refused her from the outset. The early family scenes reveal the harshness of the maternal tie. Madame Simonin presents to her daughter only the image of the punitive mother, cold as stone. She mirrors the coldness of the wintry setting that might have made a rapprochement easier, by effacing the mother's own glacial distance: "It was winter time. She was sitting in an armchair in front of the fire, she had a stern expression, stared straight in front of her and her features remained rigid. I went up to her, threw myself at her feet and begged forgiveness for all the wrong things I had done" (39).

Diderot's text does not fully exploit the cruelty of this scene, but in Suzanne's questioning we hear an anguished inner cry: "But I am still your child, you have carried me in your womb, and I hope that you will not forget that." "'Mother,' I said, 'give me back your love and physical presence, restore to me the affection of the man who thinks he is my father'" (39). The daughter goes so far as to reenact a birthing, in reverse: the uterine blood flows from the daughter to the mother:

> I got into a carriage in which I found my mother waiting for me alone. I took the seat in front and the carriage set off. We sat opposite each other for some time without a word, my eyes were lowered and I dared not look at her. I don't know what went on in my innermost soul, but suddenly I flung myself at her feet and laid my head on her knees, saying nothing, but sobbing and gasping for breath. She pushed me away roughly. I did not get up, my nose began to bleed, I nevertheless seized one of her hands and made it wet with mingled tears and blood as I kissed it, saying: "You are still my mother and I am still your child." . . . My tears and the blood from my nose mingled together and ran down my arms, and I had it all over me before I noticed. I gathered from the few words she said that her dress and underclothes had been stained and that it annoyed her. (34)

This incestuous and homosexual desire for attachment to the mother creates two situations in the novel. Suzanne cannot help hating whoever comes between her and her mother: on the one hand, her (false) father, Monsieur Simonin; and on the other, the unknown father, actually a phantasm of the real father. In this particular situation the absence of the father thus becomes something desired, for it allows an unrestricted emotional outpouring toward the mother: "Your father is away and you have plenty of time to say what you want" (39). His return is enough for the feared severance—a veritable weaning—to be carried out punitively: "Monsieur Simonin came in. He loved his wife, he saw the state she was in, he was a violent man. He stopped dead, gave me a terrible look and said: 'Leave this room!'" (42).

Suzanne's descriptions of her father must always be read with an eye for their phantasmatic dimension—the sudden apparition, the piercing gaze, the theatrical menace that make up the frightful scenario. This element of phantasm is especially evident in one of the most mysterious scenes of the novel, the scene that closes the family episode. There, the father appears as a veritable sorcerer. Suzanne gives him a ghostly aspect in his dressing-gown and nightcap. We seem to witness a mock scene of seduction, with the sudden appearance of the false father in the night, the look of terror, and the theatricality of Monsieur Simonin's threat. Suzanne's rejection of paternity is experienced as a fantasized rape:

> one morning at nine my door opened suddenly; it was Monsieur Simonin, in his dressing gown and nightcap. Since I had known that he was not my father his presence had filled me with terror. I jumped up and curtseyed. At that moment I felt as though I had two hearts. I could not think of my mother without emotion and wanting to cry, but that was far from the case with Monsieur Simonin. What is certain is that a father inspires a kind of emotion one has for nobody else, but you don't appreciate this until you have found yourself, as I did, with a man who has fulfilled that august function for a long time and has just ceased to do so. And nobody else will ever understand what it means. If I went from his presence to my mother's I felt a different person. (43)

For Suzanne, the mother is the primary relation. Suzanne's original deprivation throws her into despair and turns her into a severed being, wandering from one space to another: it is impossible for her to be integrated into the family structure; relations within the space of the convent are abnormal; when she leaves the convent, Suzanne once again finds herself in the company of libertines and matrons. Her itinerary relentlessly follows the path of her original separation. In the *Préface-Annexe* letters, as Suzanne lies on her death-bed despairing of ever finding another family, what takes shape in her visions is the mother-daughter relation. A family scene springs up before her, and the orphan appeals to Madame Madin:

> [Suzanne] sought my hand, I gave it to her; she took it, brought it up to her lips, and drawing me toward her, asked me, so quietly that I could barely hear her:
> "Mother, one more favor."
> "What would you like, my child?"
> "That you bless me and then leave."
> She added: "Don't forget to thank . . . Monsieur the Marquis."

However, the longed-for paternal adoption will be denied Suzanne all the way up to her death: indeed, this lack in some sense provokes her death, as, according to anecdote, Diderot decides to "kill off" his protagonist when the idea of attracting the Marquis de Croismare, her benefactor, to Paris to save her is unsuccessful. But when Madame Madin gives Suzanne her hand, the utterance of symbolic filiation is whispered, stifled by her last dying breath.[2]

For the Love of God

The convents in *The Nun*—beginning with Longchamp, Suzanne's first—function as a seductive apparatus, divulging new initiations at every turn.[3] Readers have tended to overlook in Madame de Moni, who first welcomes Suzanne, the sexual overtones they willingly attribute to the mother superior of Arpajon, Suzanne's third convent. The sweet Madame de Moni is viewed solely as a maternal figure. But one would have to be blind or prudish—or both—not to see that Madame de Moni is the first person to train on Suzanne a seduction mixed with devotion and mystery. In particular, the prayer scenes with Madame de Moni and Suzanne inevitably end up partaking of seduction. Suzanne herself initially denies the seduction but ends up admitting to it: "Yet her object was not seduction, but that is what she achieved" (47). Madame de Moni sets up a whole physiological system of seduction that Suzanne, through imitation, allows herself to fall into: "Her thoughts, expressions and parables went straight to your very heart. At first you listened, then little by little you were borne along, you were one with her, your soul thrilled and you shared her ecstasy" (47). The mother superior deploys a thorough and complex understanding of the organs and their sensual reactions, and she communicates this sympathetic sensuality to Suzanne:

> It was an impress that came upon her and remained a long time with her, and we kept it too. For I am not basing this on my experience alone, but that of all the nuns. Some of them have told me that they felt a longing for consolation spring up within them like the desire for a great pleasure, and I think I might have reached that state myself had I grown more accustomed to the experience. (47–48)

Another name for these states of sensual awakening is melancholy—a sort of meandering of the senses, an imaginary state between tears and ecstasy. As for the desire for union, it too has another name: consolation—an apparently desexualized (sublimated) form of union, yet one that does not fail to procure "a great pleasure" (48). Suzanne quickly learns her mother superior's lessons, and soon a remarkable reversal takes place in the story: Madame de Moni begins to imitate Suzanne. The seduction turns back on itself; this time, the seductress finds herself seduced. Before long, Suzanne herself decides when to visit the mother superior; she becomes the one who initiates pleasure: "One day when I was more perplexed and downcast than ever, I went to her cell" (48). "On the eve of my profession I went to see her" (48). In this encounter their positions are dramatically reversed. The characters are steeped in erotic confusion, but it is sublimated by the aesthetic aspect of the tableau: "her melancholy was equal to mine. I began to weep and so did she" (49). It would seem from what follows that Madame de Moni has fallen headlong into her own trap. We have only to penetrate the restraint of the text to recognize the unmistakable sexual tone of the following scene (Madame de Moni's ejaculatory climax), the apparent denial of sexuality notwithstanding. The mother superior speaks as follows:

> I have not come to talk to you, but to see you and listen to what you have to say . . . try not to upset me, but let my emotions build up within me, and when I can contain no more I will leave you. I must stay quiet. I know myself, and I act on the first impulse, but it is violent and I don't want it to work itself off on you. Just rest a little longer and let me look at you, just say a few words and let me find here what I have come to look for. (50)

The older nun's meditative posture—her false passivity—offers a veritable pantomime of seduction. She forces Suzanne into the spectator's position, into an attitude of sensual, passive receptivity. The stage is set to bring their bodies up to an optimal level of excitation but also to maintain the distance between them. Each faces the other but, like the image in a mirror, remains unattainable, phantasmatic, a mere reflection to be admired. The eroticism of the scene is expressed through looks and bodily emanations—breath, tears, swoons. Suzanne recounts it thus: "I fell silent, lay back on my pillow and held out one hand to her, which she took. She seemed to be meditating, and meditating deeply. She kept her eyes tightly shut, but now and again opened them, looked heavenwards and then back at me; she became agitated, her soul was troubled, recovered its calm and then grew troubled again" (50).

Given the extravagance of such a scene, we can easily understand why Madame de Moni asks to be excused from Suzanne's undressing, admitting that it "would distract [her] attention" (68). God clearly appears in these episodes as an imaginary place, as the very locus of seduction. This is both what unites the nuns (hence the seductiveness of prayer sessions in particular, as occasions of bodily convergence) and what separates them. Their passionate drive is directed toward this third party, toward this exclusive locus of phantasm. But the very extravagance of this phantasmatic representation opens it to desire. Desire is revealed in all its brutality when the phantasm can no longer absorb it. This is what happens to Madame de Moni when she says that God withdraws. In the end it is Suzanne who fascinates her, who has a Medusa-like effect on her and who occupies the entire space of Moni's desire. Hence their *pas de deux*, a dance of presence and absence, of mutual distancing only to be more present to each other: "'I don't know,' she said, 'what is happening to me. It seems that when you come to me, God withdraws and my spirit falls silent, and in vain I try to work myself up, I hunt for ideas and seek to lift up my heart. I find I am just an ordinary woman and an insignificant one, and I am afraid to say anything'" (48). Suzanne responds, as if she herself could not be the cause of this silence: "'Ah, dear Mother,' I said, 'what a presentiment! Suppose it were God making you silent!'" (48).

Suzanne's desire to find maternal consolation in Madame de Moni extends to the desire to resemble her. Suzanne's mimetic perversion becomes evident in what Madame de Moni taught her to do best: pray. The effort to resemble the mother superior is first of all an act of self-seduction. Suzanne imitates the model of her desire, but in miming Madame de Moni's seduction, she is also able to borrow the mother superior's power to fascinate others:

> I don't think I have ever addressed God with more fervour and received more consolation; my heart palpitated violently and in a moment I lost all consciousness of anything round me. I don't know how long I stayed in that position or how long I might have stayed, but apparently I was a very touching sight to my companion and to the two nuns when they came. When I rose I

> thought I was alone, but I was mistaken, for the three of them were behind me and weeping. . . . When I turned back towards them the expression on my face must have been awe-inspiring to judge from the effect produced upon them at the time and from what they said later, namely that I looked like our former Superior [Madame de Moni] . . . and that my appearance had filled them with the same awe. (71)

Prayer reveals Suzanne's desire for a filial relation with Madame de Moni—to the extent that, beyond the physical sympathy they share, as we have seen, there is also an ultimate union of souls. The two characters are like extensions of each other. This confusion is also the fascination Suzanne holds for the superior. The text shows these mirroring effects as if the same gift of speech had been bestowed on them, as if an outside force had arranged their words and had brought them into this divine homophony. This intimate desire for resemblance is so strong that it not only makes each of them the other's model, or hypostasis; it also leads to a public unveiling of their secrets:

> It is true that I found it extremely easy to share her ecstasy, and when she prayed aloud I sometimes took up what she had said, went on with the thread of her thoughts and found as if by inspiration part of what she would have said herself. The others listened in silence or followed on what she had said, but I interrupted or even anticipated her or spoke with her. The impress I had taken from her remained stamped on me for a long time, and it seems that I must have given some of it back to her; for if it was clear in others that they had been conversing with her, it was also clear in her that she had been conversing with me. (71–72)

Suzanne wields a diabolical power of fascination over the mother superior. She is perfectly aware of her effect on Madame de Moni: "I don't know what had been happening inside her, whether I had filled her with misgivings about her own strength which never left her again, whether I had made her self-conscious, or whether I had really broken her communication with God" (48). Suzanne's passivity, her inaction, makes her all the more dangerous. She performs the same sort of unconscious seduction that we saw in Marianne. In Suzanne's case, her "action at a distance," as Nietzsche would have called it,[4] is sublimated through mysticism. The mother superior's death must be viewed as the exaggerated effect of Suzanne's presence on her. Suzanne fulfills the fatal function of the *fascinum* as Lacan described it: "it is what has the effect of stopping movement and literally taking life."[5] Madame de Moni is inhabited by Suzanne's image, to the point of madness. How else are we to interpret the emotional upheaval of the mother superior, her mad rounds through the halls, her doleful mortifications of the flesh, all the activity she imposes on herself while Suzanne sleeps peacefully?

Finally, at the end of this impossible voyage, God is able to return. Madame de Moni's death, the return of her seductive voice, coincides with Suzanne's imaginary effacement, the exorcism of her diabolical presence. The relief provided by the superior's death allows the entire community, having been neglected because of the intoxicating attention exclusively directed toward Suzanne, at last to gather before her once again: "'Draw near, all of you, and let me kiss you, come and receive my blessing and farewell'" (53).

A Curiosity That Kills

The seductive machine is deployed to its greatest effect at Arpajon. One thing is certain, however: the sublimating mysticism of Longchamp is nowhere to be found at Arpajon. Here seduction shows its true colors: the act is unmistakable and the object precise. Although Suzanne submits to her mother superior's advances (which are frequent from the time of Suzanne's arrival at the convent), it must be admitted that she brings to these scenes of seduction a certain amount of curiosity—a supplement that leaves some doubt as to her emphatically proclaimed innocence. These doubts about Suzanne's innocence appear when certain episodes in the novel are juxtaposed: for example, the two parts of the great orgasm scene with the mother superior. First, Suzanne witnesses the mother superior's orgasm: "she went as pale as death, closed her eyes, and her whole body tautened violently, her lips were first pressed together and moistened with a sort of foam, then they parted and she seemed to expire with a deep sigh" (137–38). Later, Suzanne collaborates with her to produce the same pleasure: "I went over to her and she once again motioned me to sit on her lap, which I did; she was half dead and I felt as though I were dying myself. . . . However, the good Superior . . . was still lying back in her chair and her eyes were still closed, but her face was lit up with the loveliest colour" (138).

Leading up to this scene is the "little music lesson" that doubles as a blithe object lesson in anatomy: "Then I played some pieces of Couperin, Rameau and Scarlatti, during which she lifted a corner of my collar and rested her hand on my bare shoulder, with the tips of her fingers touching my breast" (134). Suzanne's comment: "We were enjoying ourselves in a manner as simple as it was pleasant" (135). Just as before, the erotic relationship needs an outside force to facilitate it, but music has the power to unite, whereas prayer, as a sublimated form, impedes total merging.

Let us consider these anatomy lessons, these laboratory exercises that invite the participation of the entire body. The whole of bodily space is involved in this appeal to the senses. Such anatomical exhaustiveness (reminiscent of Sade) returns at several places in the narrative: "always a kiss on the forehead or neck, eyes, cheeks, mouth, hands, bosom or arms, but most often on the mouth, for she thought I had sweet breath, white teeth and fresh ruby lips" (133–34). An even better example: "The hand she had rested on my knee wandered all over my clothing from my feet to my girdle, pressing here and there" (137).

Suzanne's innocence is hardly compromised by these scenes. But it must be said that she does more than naively consent: she willingly repeats and relives this newly discovered pleasure through her memories. In the case of her relations with

Madame de Moni, Suzanne looked forward to the moment of sexual contact; at Arpajon, pleasure is also sought in recollection, relived in solitude. Suzanne awakens from this daydream in time to discover her new "malady." The melancholy of the mystical scenes has now become the pure meandering of desire. There is also a new objectivation of Suzanne's sexual desire that neither devotion nor prayer can cover up any longer and that can be explained by the subject's dispersion under the threat of Eros. Suzanne is plunged into a sort of libidinal distraction; the sexual object seems to be everywhere and nowhere, wild and impossible to hold: "I wanted to pray but could not; I tried to find something to do and began one task and gave it up for another . . . my hands stopped of their own accord and I was so to speak stupid—I had never experienced anything like it. My eyes closed in spite of me and I fell into a little doze, although I never usually sleep in the daytime" (140).

Some of the passages leave even less doubt concerning Suzanne's consent. When the mother superior proposes to touch her one night, she answers: "Dear Mother, you need not be afraid of that" (150); later in the same scene, offering to warm up the superior, Suzanne is quite willing to open her nightdress and to repeat her superior's actions one after the other. Suzanne's mimeticism (she gives to the thing she desires the contagious name of "illness") should not blind us to what lies behind the obedience expected of her: her own dissimulated demands, her own timid desires.[6] Walter Benjamin describes (in the context of Goethe's *Elective Affinities*, to which I shall return) the sort of false veneer of innocence that lies in wait for Suzanne. This is how he explains its duplicitous functioning: "What passes for a sign of interior purity is precisely, at the same time, what concupiscence welcomes most eagerly. The innocence of not-knowing is no less equivocal, since, contrary to all expectations, it is out of not-knowing that inclination evolves into a desire that is considered guilty."[7]

In the scene that follows, Suzanne puts herself in a maieutic position, seeming to exclude herself from the mother superior's pleasure by generously according her a monopoly on desire ("I was only too glad to add to her happiness" [137]). But it would be wrong to view the mother superior simply as an aggressor, a role reinforced by her function as initiator. In actuality the roles are much more fluid: active and passive behaviors are constantly, surreptitiously changing places. In the scene just cited the narration changes its "subject." The description is occupied no longer by the body that receives pleasure but by the body that offers it. The gift is transformed into an offering. We find Suzanne entwined, entangled, merged in the pleasure that she helped to create: "I kissed her again on forehead, cheeks, eyes and lips. The hand she had rested on my knee wandered all over my clothing" (137).

Suzanne fights off any kind of sexual awakening: in a paranoid refusal to accept it in her own body, she projects it onto others as aggression or contagion. Sexuality, for Suzanne, must come only from the outside. Her innermost self cannot be violated by these obscure flurries that remain outside the control of her will. This is why Suzanne reacts in terror to her moments of solitude. These libidinal stirrings invade her body out of the blue, taking hold of her by surprise: "Why could I neither pray nor get on with anything? . . . Why should I, who have never slept in the daytime, feel myself drifting off into slumber? I thought it must be some contagious illness which was beginning to take effect on me" (166–67). This unbidden arrival of sexuality, this invasion, is all the more dangerous for the individual because it strikes in solitude.[8] Suzanne must appropriate *jouissance* into her own body, no longer externalizing it as a spectacle belonging to the other. Solitary *jouissance* could lead to even more perverse acts than lesbian eroticism:

> Of course I am not a man, and I don't know what can be imagined about one woman and another, still less about one woman alone, but as my bed had no curtains and people came in and out of my room at all hours, what can I say, Sir? For all their circumspect behaviour, their modest eyes and the chastity of their talk, these women must be very corrupt at heart—anyway they know that you can commit indecent acts alone, which I don't know. (86)

Another seduction scene that could be cited reveals the mother superior's sexual imagination, her phallic behavior, more than it does any sexual apprenticeship:

> "Now tell, me, what impression does a man's presence make on you? . . . Suzanne, do you sleep well? . . . Do you go to sleep at once?"
> "Most often."
> ". . . You don't like just dreaming? . . . Enjoying the lovely warmth of the bed? . . . You have never been tempted to consider with some self-satisfaction how beautiful you are?" (145–47)

This is an interesting strategy on the part of the mother superior, who, to command Suzanne's attention, begins by presenting a man as the imaginary partner in the sexual relation and then presents the advantages of solitary pleasure. But in order to complete her seduction of Suzanne, the mother superior will place her in front of the specular trap, flattering her narcissism. Thus, the sexual object is first normalized (as a man); then it is perverted into fetishism, alighting on various objects (pillow, bed); and finally it culminates in a narcissistic, masturbatory reflection: "It has never occurred to you to run your hands over that lovely bosom, those legs, that body, that firm, soft, white flesh of yours?" (147). This is a false narcissistic projection, however, because it hopes to elicit the other's acceptance through flattery. Once the subject is fulfilled, the other may approach.

Diderot invests these episodes with an aesthetic significance. They unfurl before our eyes like a series of tableaux. In the case of Madame de Moni, ecstatic beatitude is portrayed in the most glowing colors: "She seemed to be meditating, and meditating deeply. She kept her eyes tightly shut, but now and again opened them, looked heavenwards and then back at me; she became agitated, her soul was troubled, recovered its calm and then grew troubled again" (50). Diderot's brush also lingers over the mother superior of Arpajon: "She was still lying back in her chair and her eyes were still closed, but her face was lit up with the loveliest colour" (138).

Although the novel presents the lesbian episode as a narrative catastrophe, nevertheless it paradoxically sustains a kind of aesthetic gratification (perhaps a voyeuristic one) that softens the catastrophe. Even if Diderot presents lesbian confinement as a deviation from the "normal" sexual economy (the convent paradoxically metaphorizes the impossibility of the homosexual relation),[9] it would seem that the author himself participates in the *jouissance* of this deviation. The atmosphere at the Arpajon convent is certainly very gay: laughter, liqueurs and singing are daily fare in this enchanting establishment. But the mother superior of Arpajon, the homosexual figure in the story, takes her place in the gallery of Diderot's finest characters. Her remarkable resemblance to Rameau's nephew, Diderot's tormented musician-hero, is visible in her colorful constitution and chaotic behavior: "she wriggles on her chair . . . she is sometimes familiar to the point of my-dearing you, and sometimes haughty and imperious to the point of disdain . . . she is in turn compassionate and hard. . . . Her ever-changing expression indicates the disconnectedness of her mind and all the instability of her character" (121–22).

We must compare this agitated weathervane of a superior with the impassive Suzanne: "How gentle your pulse is! and regular! Nothing upsets it" (149). The very rigid Suzanne is not at all Diderotesque, but the tumultuous superior of Arpajon is quintessentially so. It is quite fitting, then, that this mercurial, meterological mother superior should finish in lightning: "She saw God, the heavens seemed rent with lightnings, opening and rumbling above her head, angels descended in wrath and the eye of the Lord made her tremble" (180).

It would seem that, as with Madame de Moni, Suzanne's powers of fascination are also what drive the superior of Arpajon to her death. Although Suzanne is passive at the beginning and submits to the superior's immoderate passions, the situation eventually changes. As at Longchamp, Suzanne's presence is enough to effect changes in her milieu. The superior soon stops making her rounds; her immoderate urges abate into tranquility: "The community had never been happier than since I had joined it. The superior seemed to have lost her moody character and *they said I had steadied her*" (147; emphasis added). The superior subsequently "began to give way to restlessness and she lost her gaiety, freshness and sleep" (147).

Seduction kills. The superstitious accusation on the part of Suzanne's final mother superior, that she had "cast spells over [her] predecessor" (183), would be justified in this context. But we must view this death as an excess of fascination, as an imaginary possession of the desired object—the culmination of the imaginary absorption of the object desired. What the seducer desires is to occupy the other's locus of desire, to be inhabited by the other. Suzanne remarks quite rightly that even in her moments of madness the superior "never made a mistake and took somebody else for me" (180).[10] The mother superior's shivers are both the expression of her loss of ego and the somatic projection of Suzanne's coldness toward her. The moment Suzanne approaches with kindness, everything changes: "'Oh my dear, see how my feet have warmed up at once because there is nothing between them and yours'" (151). The fatal lightning that besets the superior at her death—a deliverance from her fascination with Suzanne—must be viewed as the final projection, the virtual ejaculation, of a climax that up to this point has been denied her.

Suzanne's relations with the mothers can be read anew in terms of mediation. Those figures who are unable to resemble the maternal model become corrupting, persecuting, or obstructive models. Suzanne's perversion consists in forcing the superiors into her ideal maternal mediation (Madame de Moni is the only one who succeeds). This is exactly what she plays out in front of Sister Sainte-Christine. Suzanne describes with malicious pleasure how she brought to life the image of Sainte-Christine's predecessor:

> The first thing I did was to give myself up to all the grief I felt at the loss of our first Superior, and sing her praises on every occasion, make comparisons between her and our present ruler which were unfortunate for the latter, describe the state of the convent in previous years, call back to mind the peace we used to enjoy, the kindly treatment we had, the food, both spiritual

> and material, we used to be given, and laud to the skies the way of life, sentiments and character of Sister de Moni. (55–56)

The fate of the mother superior at Sainte-Eutrope is even more cruel. This rejected mother, put in her place by the daughter, does not even come close to the maternal ideal. She is not like Madame de Moni, the endearing image, the figure of plenitude: "I could not help comparing her with my first Superior. What a difference! There was neither the same piety, nor the same seriousness, nor dignity, nor fervour, nor intelligence, nor sense of order" (168). To the contrary, her threatening image flashes in Suzanne's face, a demonic expression of desire. This is how she appears in one of Suzanne's hallucinations: "I stopped, turned and looked at her again and saw that I had been terrified by a strange effect of my own imagination: her position in relation to the church lamp had been such that only her face and the tips of her fingers had been lit up, the rest was in shadow, and that had given her a weird appearance" (165).

The catastrophe of relations in *The Nun* signals the exhaustion of endogamous mediation, the subject's frustration in finding the ideal model for herself. As for the lesbian relation—a union that is both desired and impossible—it is the exacerbated form that mediation takes in its original homosexual yearning for the mother. It repeats the torment of the separation from the mother, of that original denial.

Siren

The nun performs her seduction above all through her voice. The melodious power of her singing is irresistible. At Longchamp, "simply by force of habit because I knew it so well, I sang *Tristes apprêts*. . . . I don't know what effect that produced, but they didn't listen for long: I was interrupted by praises" (45). Suzanne does not hesitate to pervert the celebration of the Passion into a vehicle for her vocal seduction, for bringing her unhappy destiny to the attention of the community. She herself recognizes the profanity of her theatrics. But she transfers the diabolical scandal (*skandalon*) of her action onto the crowd: "I sang well enough to provoke tumultuous bursts of that scandalous applause they give to actors in their theatres, and which should never be heard in the house of the Lord, above all during those solemn and mournful days when we honour the memory of His Son nailed to the Cross in atonement for the sins of all mankind" (68).

And again: "I sang and played the organ and was applauded" (72). Music and singing are what unite. They will be enlisted in Suzanne's ultimate attempts to find a family, in the *Préface-Annexe*. She suggests to the Marquis: "I have a good voice and am musical, and I can play the harpsichord well enough to entertain any mother who would like me to, and I could even give lessons to her children."[11] This seduction by voice even enters the level of the narrative; Suzanne is enchanting in spite of the silence that writing imposes on her. She is anxious to present herself in the best light to the recipient of her Mémoires, the Marquis de Croismare: "I am of a very strange cast of mind: when things could inspire your respect or add to your sympathy I write well or ill, but with incredible speed and facility; I feel gay in heart, expressions come easily to me, I am easily moved to tears and I seem to feel your presence and see you there listening to me" (178).

The ambiguous nature of seduction by writing comes out at the end of her Mémoires, and as an excuse Suzanne begs the ambiguity of her entire sex. She refers to the impossibility of feminine pathos or suffering, as if women were reduced solely to the pleasure principle, to their charms. But wouldn't woman's pathos be viewed by the masculine imagination as hardly different from her euphoria or narcissistic rejoicing? In both cases, feminine expressivity seeks recognition from the other sex. The sensual, passionate truth of woman is for man first and foremost a spectacle: the terms that Suzanne lights on are a picture of troubles (to move the heart) and a portrait of charms (to seduce):

> I have noticed that without the slightest intention I had shown myself in every line, certainly as unhappy as I was, but much

> more attractive than I am. Could it be that we think men are less affected by a picture of our troubles than by a portrait of our charms? And do we count on it being easier to seduce them than to touch their hearts? I have too little experience of them, and I have not studied them sufficiently to know. And yet supposing the Marquis, who is reputed to be the most delicate of men, were to persuade himself that I am addressing myself not to his charity but to his lust, what would he think of me? This thought worries me. In reality he would be quite mistaken if he ascribed to me in particular an instinct common to all my sex. I am a woman, and perhaps a bit coquettish, who can tell? But it is a result of our nature, and not of artifice on my part. (189)

This having been said, Suzanne can go as far as the indecency of seduction; like Marivaux's heroine, she tries to excuse her behavior through unconscious movements, feigned gestures that show off her body to advantage: "I was trying to readjust my veil, but my hands were shaking, and the more I tried to put it right the more I upset it" (78). To be eroticized, the adorned body must be made to shine a little; the glimmer of naked flesh must be held out:

> by dint of tugging they broke the thread in some places, the veil or my dress was torn in others, and I could be seen. . . . I have a striking face; my great suffering had changed it but had taken nothing from its character. I have a voice which touches the heart and my expression bears the stamp of truthfulness. The combination of these qualities made a strong impression of pity on the two young acolytes. (94)

One would think that Suzanne was continually forced into exhibiting herself; there is always a hand to strip off her veil. But the effect on others is always as much for their benefit as it is for hers. The removal of the veil seems like a rape of her body; but with Suzanne's hesitation, we are unable to tell if it is a phantasm or simply a projection proving the innocence of her unconscious exhibitionism: "so I undressed, or rather my veil and clothes were torn off me" (110).

Suzanne's narcissistic pretenses must be mentioned in this

context. As is the case with her erotic behavior, these pretenses fully assert themselves only after the fact, when the dreaded complicity of solitude allows her gleefully to take stock of her experiences:

> My companions surrounded me, embraced me, saying to each other: 'Just look, Sister, isn't she lovely! . . . How well that band suits her!' . . . I scarcely took in what they were saying, for I was overcome with grief. And yet I must confess that when I was alone in my cell I recalled their flattering remarks and couldn't resist verifying them in my little mirror, and I felt they were not altogether undeserved. (25)

Sleep, whose maternal aspect we have seen in the company of Madame de Moni, is also one of these narcissistic, eroticized states.[12] These moments when the subject is wrapped up in herself, with a self-absorption that feigns self-forgetfulness, are clearly auto-affectivity, self-indulgence. Suzanne's fainting spells, her forgetfulness, her unconscious poses, losses of consciousness, blackouts, daydreams, absent-mindedness—all of the subject's "innocent" moments of interiority—contribute to her making a spectacle of herself, to showing the artifice and the theatricality of her absence.

Even when she assumes the position of the victim, Suzanne captures the locus of desire, that of the divine image. At Longchamp she becomes the focus of the sisters' prayers. She occupies the place of the object of worship, at the center of the religious community's desires. All masses are henceforth sung for her. In these painful scenes of mortification—these inverted rites—Suzanne, paradoxically, is exactly where she desires to be: in the middle of the choir, at the center of attention.

Suzanne, too, is a virtuous erotomaniac.

Part 2

Initiations

The Seductive Parasite

Marivaux, *The Upstart Peasant*

Jacob's seduction could be described as passive: it works like a kind of magnetism.[1] Jacob's presence alone scintillates and fascinates. His body and bearing combined are the immediate force that attracts and inaugurates the moment of seduction. Throughout the novel, Jacob is presented as an apparition, primarily something that is seen and desired: "The pleasure of seeing myself" (10);[2] "it was only necessary to have eyes to find me attractive. . . . I was a handsome man, I was well built, I had natural graces, and all this at the first glance" (132). In any case, he certainly provokes unanimous desire in those who come into contact with him:

> each one uttered his remark upon my appearance, and happily, of all these comments, there was not one by which I could be offended; there were even some very obliging ones from the women. "He doesn't have the manner of a fool," said one . . . "he is a handsome boy," said another. . . . In short I can say that my road was strewn with compliments. (95)

Jacob is the adored phallus. Among the epithets applied to him are "little man," "my handsome child," "bigwig." It is not so much Jacob who is desired by women, as it is the phallus itself, through him. Women dress him up, making him into their ideal object.[3] The first of these ladies has his measurements taken by the tailor of the house and thus transforms him into the object of her phantasy: "Two days later my suit was brought to me with linen, a hat, and all the rest of my attire. A footman of the house who had taken a liking to me curled my hair; I had rather good hair" (10). Emboldened, Jacob shows off his new charms: "The lady then bade me come closer and examined my finery. . . . She asked me who had curled my hair and told me always to be careful about my hair, that it was beautiful" (10–11). Later it will be Mademoiselle Habert's turn to dress him up according to her fancy, to adorn him with her dreams, and even to endow him a phallic pretension that he seemed to lack on his own, in order to perfect his proud erection:

> "And apropos of a man's costume, my little wife," I said to her, "there is a trifle that I have always longed for. . . ." "Why, what is it, my friend?" she replied. "Only a sword and belt," I said, "to make me Monsieur de la Vallée in good earnest; nothing sets off the figure so much, and besides, with that, all gentlemen are your equals." (130)

Jacob's dressing scene is also a spectacle worth the sight:

> When the suit was purchased, an amorous impatience seized my wife to see me all equipped; "my boy," said she, "let us go at once to find a sword-belt, stockings, a hat . . . a new ready-made shirt, and all the trimmings, shan't we?"
> "As you please," said I, with a gaiety that was heartfelt; and as soon said as done; all the shop-keepers were summoned . . . and before dinner-time I had the joy of seeing Jacob metamorphosed into a cavalier with the silk lining, with the genteel silver edging on the hat, and the adornment of a head of hair that hung down to the waist on which the hair-dresser had exhausted all his skill. (132)

Jacob's narcissism exists only as a projection of female desire. One scene in particular shows the true nature of this narcissism. It is in the coquette's mirror that Jacob becomes aware of his charms. This scene shows the coincidence (the jubilant refraction) of two narcissisms: "she sat down again to her toilette, and as for me, I left but still turning around to gaze at her. Nor did she lose sight of what I did and followed me to the door with her eyes" (11–12). Jacob can thus pass from one woman to another ("The phallus is a wanderer," writes Lacan[4]); he inspires unanimity in women's phantasms, and women, reciprocally, are the models, the instigators of his desire.

Jacob represents the ultimate point of convergence for the female imaginary: women never seem to be jealous of each other in this novel. Mademoiselle Habert herself, Jacob's wife, shows little of it. The presence of the phallic object is enough to satisfy her: "Mme de la Vallée, all loving as she is, is not in the least jealous. . . . If I am absent, Mme de la Vallée wishes ardently for my return but waits in peace; when she sees me again? No question; there she is, delighted" (196). Nor should this lack of possessive jealousy be attributed to Jacob's discretion, to the stealth of his seductive techniques. In fact, Madame de Fécour can invite him in front of Madame de Ferval, and Madame de Ferval in front of Mademoiselle Habert herself: "He will come alone," she insists before Jacob's wife, who attempts in vain to obstruct this lovers' tryst. These amorous encounters clarify the nature of Jacob's seduction. It is always in other women (through the intermediary of another woman) that he is appropriated, like an object ready and waiting to be offered to the desire of the other.

Contrary to what one might think, *The Upstart Peasant* is a female novel. In it, as in *Marianne*, women constitute a sort of community that is a hotbed of mimetic activity. What must be read behind mentions of physical resemblance is the mimetic temptation or the value as mimetic object par excellence that Jacob represents. He is the object of all desires—such is always the essence of the seducer:

> [CATHERINE:] "Look, you are as like as two drops of water to my departed Baptiste whom I had thought to marry . . . and a handsome young fellow like you." (38)

> [MADAME DE FÉCOUR:] "The first man for whom I ever felt an inclination was just like you." (146)

> [MADAME D'ALAIN:] "What a handsome head! . . . if ever I marry I shall take a man who has one like it." (133)

Jacob is essentially interchangeable. Even his beautiful clothing, through unlikely circumstances, is made from someone else's measurements: "M. Simon bowed to me, looked at me. 'By my faith,' said he, 'there needn't be the trouble of acquiring the cloth; I have in my shop a brand new suit . . . and the man for whom it was made has left it with me for recompense . . . I think it will be just right for Monsieur'" (131).

This principle of interchangeability remains the same even if we change our reading perspective: in the economic order, Jacob is a commodity on the market, evaluated in terms of the general equivalent. He is continually appraised, priced, and exchanged for favors by women. In the symbolic order, he is the phallus.[5] He is the envy of all the world, the possessor of desire.[6] The seducer is passed from one woman to another, with a playful contentment that flatters him. He is like the slipper in the singing-game, "the wooden slipper passed by here, my Ladies." Jacob's seduction, then, is passive; it is somehow coextensive with his being. Seduction, whetted by rumor, beats him to it, one might say: herein resides his "obscenity." What motivates Jacob constantly to participate in seduction is the recognition, the flattery it bestows upon his vanity (*amour-propre*: literally "self-love"). With Madame de Ferval, Jacob "simply was charmed to find myself attractive to a great lady. . . . I shouldn't have taken notice of her if she hadn't taken notice of me. . . . I saw . . . a woman, in a word, who raised us, my vanity and me, from their original worthlessness" (109).

Jacob makes it clear that the real object is a secondary motivation for his seduction. What counts more than anything is the narcissistic reflex, the phantasmatic satisfaction of the ego, the taste of successfully recollecting the seductive adventure. At every instant of his seduction, Jacob is inhabited by male vanity: "I was in love, then, from respect and from astonishment at my adventure, from the intoxication of vanity, from whatever you please, from the infinite value I put on the charm of that lady" (110). "It was because I had perceived by one thing and another that she herself had been looking at me; that made me consider that I was a handsome young fellow" (100). Jacob's narcissism is brilliantly summed up as follows: "*Nothing makes one so amiable as to believe that one is loved*" (58, emphasis added). Narcissism, captured by the other's desire, appropriates this desire for itself and imitates it. In the genealogy of seduction that I am proposing, Jacob is a perfect representative of the first phase: He literally has no desire; his seduction consists in copying other people's desire. He modestly admits that the close attention of others allows him to rise out of a sort of "original worthlessness" of *amour-propre* (109). Vanity, for Marivaux (as we saw in Marianne's case), is an echo, a reverberation of the emptiness of the subject desirous of desire. Jacob is a kind of *tabula rasa* of desire.

The Inconstancy of Things of This World

Jacob later finds himself confronting the very trap of seduction. His libertine apprenticeship ends in a series of catastrophes. It comes as a surprise, an oddity, for him to be facing another kind of femininity. The two women who participated in his amorous education, Madame de Ferval and Madame de Fécour, are the same ones he fails to seduce—just when he believed he had gained experience. First, Madame de Ferval, after inviting him into a servant's room at Madame Remy's house, blocks the impatient advances of his unbridled youthful libido. Offering herself only to deny him, Ferval thus makes herself all the more desirable to him. Even the place she chooses is deceptive. Jacob expected an enclosure, but he finds the opposite: "people can see us through those windows" (176). The young seducer's targeted mistress is carried off before his eyes by a chevalier who bursts onto the scene; Jacob is reduced to the role of a voyeur. The only person he really wanted is contested. We can hardly take Jacob at his word when he gives Madame de Ferval's guilt as the reason for his amorous insistence; he is simply stirred up by rivalry: "it's not unusual for a guilty mistress to become more piquant" (191). In fact, it is through the chevalier that Jacob, huddled in his corner, will be able to partake of *jouissance* vis-à-vis Madame de Ferval: "you could not imagine how beautiful I found in my anger those beautiful dark eyes which he extolled" (188).

When Jacob, having lost Madame de Ferval, tries to recoup his position as seducer, he meets with disappointment once again in the person of Madame de Fécour. His former benefactress chases him out of the house after he finds her almost dying—a pose with all the appearances of hysterical symptoms. Madame de Fécour's fever may be dangerous, but the text leaves some doubt as to what the probable consequences may be. Hence, the disturbing feeling of strangeness that grows in Jacob. Thwarted, near the end of the novel he takes stock of his experiences: "The day before, I had two mistresses, or, if you prefer, two lovers; the word 'mistress' signifies too much here; commonly it means a woman who has given her heart and wishes to have yours; and the two persons of whom I speak had, I think, neither given theirs nor were anxious to have mine, which was no longer anxious for theirs" (193).

These final words convey Jacob's resignation, despite the false reciprocity of the relation. The perfumed scent of "his women" somehow lingers on in his memory. Jacob never succeeds in grasping the object of his desires. He himself tells Madame de Fécour that she was nothing but a phantasy (not only a playful adventure, but a phantasm as well). But in the act of denial and the castrating situation, he is the one left frustrated by the image. The seducer believed that he was loved, but now, in the irony and distance of the *word*, he finds himself unable to recognize the *thing*.

One role in particular interests me in these two episodes: the person who stands in the way of Jacob's two "conquests." In the case of Madame de Ferval, it is Madame Remy who plays the role of obstacle. She is the one Madame de Ferval threatens to call to put an end to Jacob's impulsive movements. In Madame de Fécour's case, a pious servant ends up chasing him away and forbids him entrance to the boudoir. In both cases, the obstructors are old women: at Madame de Ferval's house, "out came a tall elderly woman, thin, pale" (174); at Madame de Fécour's, "there was an elderly chambermaid seated at the foot of the bed . . . and it was a tall lady, ugly, thin, with a dry, severe, censorious face" (192). The figure of the old woman in these two episodes is the witch, or perhaps the punishing mother, fatally disturbing her son's desire, impeding the relation by presenting woman as an object to which he is denied access. These two old women are malefic projections of the seductress-female initiator. The witch is the guardian of secrets.

This sort of symbolic castration will take its toll on Jacob. The last attempt he makes at seduction is directed toward Madame d'Orville. But Jacob's sporting attitude has lost its edge, and he finally abandons the enterprise. The seducer returns to his family abode. The excuse he gives for his decline is a social one: it is because the chevalier who snatched Madame de Ferval away from him reminds him of his peasant origins that he has lost the confidence of the young seducer. Jacob's return to his former self is touching. It is presented as a return inward. After his past dissipation, Jacob now seeks closer contact with himself. He experiences the separation, or schism (Jacob / Monsieur de la Vallée), as a short-lived moment of happiness, of sweet *jouissance*, of infantile narcissism. The subject turns in upon himself: hunkered down in dressing-gown and slippers, he is enveloped in the warmth of his family home: "What, now, slippers and a dressing-gown for Jacob! For it was in considering myself as Jacob that I was so deliciously astonished to see myself in that dress; it was from Jacob that Monsieur de la Vallée borrowed all his joy. This moment was so sweet only because of the little peasant" (197).

As for Madame de la Vallée (the ex-Mademoiselle Habert), the narrative falls silent on her score. She is no longer even a surrogate object. We have seen that the seducer uses his spouse as an outlet for his phantasies, as a simple convenience that enables him to recapture his dreams: "my mind was filled with so many tender pictures, my heart had been fired in so many ways, and I had had love made to me so much that day, that I had been put into a humor to be amorous myself; to this add the convenience of having beside me a person who asked nothing better than to listen to me—such was Mme de la Vallée" (149).

This is the sort of imaginary orgy out of which she emerges, in all her ingenuous misrecognition. But in the end she is simply cast aside as someone no longer worthy of mention: "I shall not say another word" (196).

A Gate-crasher at the Opera

Following the bungled feminine conquests, and the boredom of the marital situation, Marivaux produces a character to whom Jacob attributes all his blessings: this is the Count d'Orsan. Their meeting is described in terms of love at first sight. It is for the count that Jacob sheds his blood. Male friendship replaces the disenchantment of female dissipation; Orsan and Jacob become inseparable through a sort of homoerotic camaraderie.

The count is a kind of narcissistic projection on Jacob's part: he is the successful, idealized seducer—the kind that Jacob, at the end of his rapidly aborted career, would have liked to be. Before Jacob's dazzled eyes, the count shines at the Opera, making a spectacle of his seduction; the young seducer is called on to imitate him, to recognize his idol, his model, in him. The count, who as a good aristocrat has internalized the art of pleasing, represents Jacob's hopes for success on the stage of Society: in him, Jacob has found his ego-ideal. Venerated, iconized, idolized by the younger man, Orsan occupies the locus of representation for Jacob. He is the neophyte's private theater, a complete one-man show. Jacob—as Monsieur de la Vallée once again—accompanies the count, acting out his charade, copying his inimitable model to the best of his abilities ("I followed him"). But bowing and scraping and put-on graces don't come naturally to him. Caught up in this mimetic whirlwind, this blinding confusion of gazes, victimized (his bows are rewarded with ridicule), and withering in the brilliance of the model, Jacob has no choice but to take refuge:

> they glanced over my singular person; and I think there was nothing so foolish as I or anything so amusing to see. The more Count d'Orsan praised me, the more he embarrassed me. I had to respond—with my little silk coat and my little bourgeois elegance, for which I no longer felt any esteem since I saw so much magnificence of dress around me. But what to reply? "Oh, nothing at all, Monsieur; you are mistaken," and then "It is a bagatelle, it is nothing; just what was necessary; I am your servant." These responses of mine I accompanied politely with short and frequent bows and scrapings to which these gentlemen apparently took a fancy, for there wasn't one among them who failed to bow to me in return. One of them whom I saw turn away to laugh made me aware of the joke and completed my humiliation; after that no more bowings; my appearance did what it could and my replies likewise. Count d'Orsan, who was a courteous man, continued to talk without taking notice of what passed with respect to me. "Let's take our places," he said to me, and I followed him. He led me onto the stage, where the number of people protected me from such affronts and where I placed myself near him like a man who takes refuge. (212)

In a psychotic mode this time, Jacob relives the dissymmetry of his birth and his desire. He falters in an imaginary moment that throws back at him the troubling, fragmented image of his uncertain ego ("my *hétéroclite* figure," 212). This split between Jacob and Monsieur de la Vallée, however, is not just a simple disjunction of the ego. In the din of the Opera, Jacob is oppressed not by Monsieur de la Vallée, that phantom of childhood dreams, but rather by the hallucination of the model, the desire for aristocracy. What dizzies Jacob is the stunning multiplication of the double-model: "so much magnificence of dress around me" (212); "the more the Count d'Orsan praised me, the more he embarrassed me" (212).

This experience places Jacob before the absolute Other at the site of *jouissance*: he is annihilated before the person who has it All. Jacob's imitative desire reveals the nothingness from which he was conceived; it exposes his unsuitability for heroism. The panic that besets him at this painful moment could be perceived as bordering on death.

The Unquiet Seducer

Crébillon, *The Wayward Head and Heart*

In *The Wayward Head and Heart*, Crébillon presents us with the different stages, the genesis, of seductive desire. Somewhat as Kierkegaard showed in the case of Don Juan, Crébillon's novel discovers three successive stages in the development of this desire. In the first phase, desire desires to externalize itself, but it remains wrapped up in itself. In the second, desire blossoms forth, but it has no particular object. The subject of desire attaches himself to anything and everything, hacking away at multiplicity. And finally, in the third stage, desire comes to know itself, resplendent in the knowledge of its own power. Ever triumphant, it allows its satisfaction to be heard.[1]

At the beginning of the *Wayward Head*, the awakening of desire is manifested in Meilcour as an impression of ennui. Although the object of desire remains imprecise, Meilcour's libidinal activity is intense. The subject finds himself in the middle of a strange conflict between inner boredom and a drive toward an external mirage-object: "I desired a felicity of which I had no very distinct idea, and for some idea I did not understand what sort of pleasure it was I stood in need of. I tried in vain to deaden the inner longing that oppressed me" (4).[2]

In this aimless casting about, desire is in fact seeking an object. Its drama is one of *choice*. Desire thus flits about, alighting here and there in an ocean of undifferentiated multiplicity:

"The matter was not without difficulties. My affections were attached to no special object, but there was no object that did not excite them; I was afraid to choose [a woman], and yet I was hardly free to do so. The feelings that one woman inspired in me were destroyed the next moment by those that another awakened" (4).

Soon to recover from this quandary, the apprentice-seducer will learn how to turn the embarassment of choices to his own advantage. Multiplicity will no longer hold the terrors that it presented when he was younger. But this embryonic stage of seduction shows the future torments that the foppish little rake will constantly seek to overcome. Seduction is a counterphobic enterprise.[3]

Meilcour's first choice reveals some interesting details that could shed considerable light on seductive desire or the compulsion to seduce. It is at the house of Madame de Meilcour—the son insists on referring thus to his mother—that he meets the object of his first amorous fixation: Madame de Lursay. Scholarly and moral pursuits give way to the pursuit of pleasure. The text of the *Wayward Head* begins with this separation from the maternal object in favor of another object of passion. Despite this expression of the body's need to exteriorize itself, the maternal closeness of the first object will always dominate Meilcour's feelings. His entire seductive enterprise could be seen as a way of proving himself to his mother, of demonstrating his phallic worth to her. The opening sentences of the *Wayward Head* sets up this familial dynamic. Madame de Meilcour's widowhood is hardly incidental to the situation: the son is constantly compelled to demonstrate that he could, ideally, replace his father:

> I made my entry into society at the age of seventeen, with all the advantages that can make a man remarkable there. My father had left me a noble name, whose lustre he himself had increased, and from my mother I had expectations of considerable wealth. Left a widow when still of an age when there were no attachments she might not have formed; young, rich, and

> handsome, her devotion to me permitted her to contemplate no other pleasure than that of educating me, and of making up to me for all that I had lost in losing my father. (3)

The mother's widowhood makes her all the more worthy of esteem; and the son prides himself on the fact that she is still desirable. The child has become his mother's sole passion. Still young, she seems to have redirected onto her son any inclination toward other attachments. The child has become a substitute, an indemnity or reparation, for the loss of the father; and his education has by her own choosing become her only pleasure. "I exist only for my mother," Meilcour seems to murmur narcissistically: *His Majesty the Baby* . . .

It is tempting therefore to read this first encounter with Madame de Lursay at the maternal home as an incestuous relation. The close ties that bind Meilcour's mother with her intimate friend make them virtually doubles of one another. Narcissistic flattery is partly responsible for determining the choice of the first sexual object—but it is also a matter, as Meilcour admits, of habit. An attachment that is completely authorized at first by maternal friendship progressively drifts or deviates toward a sexual attachment. This first knowledge of the other sex has the advantage of sparing Meilcour the "terror," the risky surprise of female difference: "Her frequent compliments upon my wit and appearance, her familiarity with me, and the habit of seeing her often, had given me a considerable affection for her and a kind of ease that I felt with no one else of her sex" (7).

Thus begins the *fort-da* game with Madame de Lursay that will end with the delightful "moment" at the end of the novel. Meilcour does indeed take pleasure in making her disappear and reappear in an imaginary game that has the effect of rendering her ever more desirable each time: "It was not that I thought I could make myself loved by her more easily than by another. So far was I from flattering myself with so charming an idea that my lack of hope of succeeding with her had often made me aspire elsewhere. But after a couple of days' infidelity I would always come back to her more tender and more timid than ever" (7).

The apprentice-seducer will later experience amorous passion for a unique object as a veritable torment. He must prove to himself that he is capable of taking his desire elsewhere: "I spent the greater part of the night reviewing in my mind all the women to whom I might form an attachment. It was labour in vain, for I found, after the most minute research, that none of them pleased me as much as Mme de Lursay" (24).

Madame de Lursay functions as a sort of midwife in the birth of the seducer. As Meilcour's initiator, she is the one who will teach him to experience the most secret pleasures. The scene of their first declaration of love reveals this maieutic relationship between Madame de Lursay and her pupil. Through a series of rhetorical detours, she leads Meilcour into a specific discourse that leaves him no choice but avowal. Countering Meilcour's refusal to give himself from the outset as the subject of the declaration, the ruse consists in inventing a third person to whom the speech is supposedly addressed, in transforming his timid performance into the subject of their talk (the declaration): "as people go on talking they change the subject so often that in the end the subject of preoccupation can naturally find a place" (11); "a declaration can only seem such an embarrassing matter because you yourself have one to make" (14). For both the apprentice-seducer and the midwife-seductress, the avowal comes as an almost erotic release: "At this unmistakable declaration of the state of my affections Mme de Lursay sighed, blushed, turned her eyes languishingly to mine. . . . My extreme efforts to drive myself on had almost overpowered me" (17).

Madame de Lursay will play this role on several occasions. Her seduction is most successful when she adopts poses of self-absorption. Her pretenses of refusing to see Meilcour, the transparent veil that she places between herself and him, only contribute to exciting the passion of her pupil even more. Her reverie—a pretense and a form of narcissistic rejection—present themselves as a veritable mimesis of desire, a pantomime of pleasure:

> During the silence that followed she seemed to be plunged in the most painful reverie. She threw me troubled glances, raised her eyes to heaven, let them fall tenderly upon me again, and seemed unable to tear them away. She kept giving heart–rending sighs, and there was something so natural and touching about her distress, she looked so lovely in her confusion, and filled me with such reverence, that if I had not already wished to please her she would surely have made me wish to do so then. (61–62)

Absorption is often represented by a typically feminine activity—embroidery: "She greeted me coldly, almost without raising her eyes from her embroidery frame" (50). Madame de Lursay is interrupted at another point in the process of "tying bows in her hair" (60). These feminine preoccupations, at times associated with reverie, threaten the seducer, inasmuch as they exclude him from a relation with the other. But through jealous male eyes, they must seem a sort of private hunting ground, an exclusively female phantasy. In the eyes of the young pupil, embroidery appears as an indecipherable sign, as an obstacle to communication and to the reciprocity of gazes. Madame de Lursay insists on the privilege of her enigma: "And I forbid you even to guess at what I leave unsaid" (37).

It would be wrong to see Madame de Lursay simply as the mediating mother, the initiator with maternal appeal. In fact, she exercises a sort of female terror over Meilcour. Alongside her erotic tenderness, she exhibits at times a sybilline severity. As much as Madame de Lursay seems to offer herself to Meilcour, she knows just as well how to refuse herself. These obstructive moments take on the general label of *respect*: this is what women hold in front of themselves like a shield, to delay the moment of possession; it is what is required of the man in the form of restraint. The respect that is shown Madame de Lursay by Meilcour is even more striking in that it takes the interiorized form of an almost filial respect on his part. This oppressive side of his relation to Madame de Lursay inevitably entails its opposite: various (and purely imaginary) wishes to humiliate her, to debase the object of love. But Madame de Lursay will always maintain that aura of veneration that Meilcour created around her during the early period of their attachment.

The desire to wean himself from this first fixation also leads him to search out other opportunities for deliverance, as in Madame de Senanges and Madame de Mongennes, who will take over Meilcour's education in pleasure in a far more efficient manner. But more than anyone it is Hortense de Théville who takes the coveted place of the desired object. When Meilcour catches sight of Hortense at the Opera he reacts as if by overflowing. His pursuit of her acts out his first true feelings of love. Chance replaces habit this time, and a public place is substituted for the maternal home. The desired object is no longer his mother's age but radiant with the freshness of youth: "Imagine the noblest attributes of the most regular beauty, the utmost charms of all the graces, in a word all that youth can radiate of freshness and brilliance" (25–26).[4]

Whereas Meilcour's attachment to Madame de Lursay implied his mother's complicity (if only through the bond of friendship linking the women), his passion for Hortense occasions the son's first confrontation with his mother over affairs of the heart. Meilcour's entire seductive career was envisaged as a way of proving himself to his mother;[5] he thus believes that "the best thing, not only for my love but also in consideration of my duty towards Madame de Meilcour, was to hide nothing from her" (108).

The maternal obstacle is at first explained by the enmity between Meilcour's mother and Hortense's mother, Madame de Théville—this at least is the excuse Meilcour anticipates: "I feared lest the antipathy that divided them might make her forbid me to see her" (108). But this antipathy is soon directed toward Hortense herself, on whom his mother's verdict falls: "'I could wish that her charms had made less impression on you than they appear to have done'" (109). The rest of the conversation becomes even more curious, and Madame de Meilcour ends up displaying outright her rivalry toward her son's object of passion: "'But Madam,' I asked her, 'would it be such a great misfortune if I loved her?' 'Yes,' she answered coldly, 'it would. Such a passion would not make you happy'" (109). There follows another ambiguous declaration: "I am glad to say I have certain plans for you, and they do not include Mademoiselle de Théville'" (109–10).

First among Men

In his preface to Crébillon's novel, Etiemble's psychoanalytic sally revealed more than even he was aware of:

> Without labelling Crébillon "pre-Freudian," we can observe that young Meilcour's fear when faced with the young and beautiful Hortense; the urge that draws him, not without fear and self-recrimination, toward a friend of his mother's who is the same age as she; the weakness that later delivers him to Senanges, a prostitute and a heartless initiator: all this makes up quite an accurate picture of an adolescent who, deprived of his father at an early age, has not settled his score with the Oedipal complex.[6]

As insightful as it is, this intuition warrants further development. If there is anyone who takes the place of the father in *The Wayward Head*, it is undoubtedly Versac. Detested by one and all, Versac is nonetheless venerated by Meilcour. In fact, the more the character is hated, the more he becomes an object of fascination for the young apprentice-seducer. He is the only character in the narrative besides Hortense who receives Meilcour's insistent attention.

Versac's first appearance in the narrative accompanies the return of the mother. In fact, it is at Madame de Meilcour's house that the son meets the initiator-model. Straightaway, in front of Versac, she displays her maternal inclination for possession. The worst thing for Meilcour's mother is to be unable to keep her son, to have to share him with other women through his initiation into libertine exchange by Versac—"the man she liked least in the world, and whom she most feared on my account. . . . She had even forbidden me to see him" (68). Versac is Meilcour's ego-ideal, the model with whom he desires to identify himself and whom he will imitate.[7] Meilcour willingly allows himself to be eclipsed behind Versac, whom he presents as the ultimate seducer; in the young man's mind, Versac takes on the lineaments of an extraordinary character, larger than life: "He combined with the highest distinction of birth the most agreeable wit and an extremely attractive appearance" (68). With all the attributes of the idealized model and the superlative qualities that make him unique, Versac is the "Hero" (French ed., 160). This uniqueness is what makes him desirable and, paradoxically, imitable. Meilcour himself falls into this trap: "There were few who did not try to imitate him, though all those who did so only made themselves less agreeable than before. It was [as] if that happy insolence was a gift of nature, which could be granted to no one but him. There could be no one like him" (68); "I never saw him without studying him and trying to make my own the sumptuous airs I admired too greatly in him" (69).

Meilcour, as narrator of the story, contrives to leave the leading role to Versac, whom he calls "the most admirable of men" (79). Meilcour himself is nothing but this narrative voice; his face is unknown to us, although we know through rumors circulated among women that his features have all the charm required of a seducer. Generally sated with the loved object, Meilcour—unlike Jacob in *The Upstart Peasant*—rarely takes the opportunity to flatter himself. Outbursts of vanity are fairly infrequent; they generally revert to moments of dispossession, of the subject in crisis. Meilcour has an almost anguished, schizophrenic need to attach himself to objects. Even the esteem in which Madame de Lursay holds him, and which is felt on several occasions in their relationship, does nothing to dispel the power she wields over him: easily rattled by her, taken unawares, he becomes a thoroughly dissipated subject.

The same cannot be said for Versac, who parades his self-sufficiency. Like the coquette, he announces his coming with fanfare: Noise precedes him, like rumor ("preceded by his customary uproar," 89). Versac has an obscene way of exteriorizing seduction, of sexualizing it by projecting it in front of himself, of allowing his affected phallic figure, his gloriously trumped-up tumescence, to be seen. He is adept at deploying all his charms: "he set out to make a display of his charms. He had a good leg: he made the most of it. He laughed as often as he could to show his teeth, and assumed the bold postures that set his figure off to best advantage and demonstrated its graces most amply" (93).

The seducer exists only through his reputation, through the words of others. If he pretends to ignore others, it is only the better to exist through them. Versac is already the conceited fop that will become familiar in nineteenth-century literature. He owes his success to a strange mimetic denial: "because everyone abhors him everyone sees him," Madame de Lursay explains insightfully (79). According to common parlance, the fop is "full of himself": it must also be pointed out that he is actually full of others. This macho version of the coquette has no more self-sufficiency than she does. In order to make himself more desirable, he must pretend not to desire. Such is the narcissistic trap that he lays.

In her book on Molière's *Don Juan*, Shoshana Felman accurately characterizes the seducer's "self-referential" desire when she writes that "the seducer holds out to women the narcissistic mirror of their own desire of themselves" (40).[8] The fop, like the coquette, carries his mirror with him; when in public he tends, while ignoring everyone else, to be the center of attention, to find his own reflexive gaze in the gaze of others.[9]

If Versac represents a sort of ego-ideal for the apprentice-seducer, he also plays a paternal role in relation to Meilcour. It is Versac who, during the eagerly awaited conversation in Part Three of the novel, will perfect Meilcour's amorous education and select his love objects for him (Mme de Senanges, Mme de Mongennes). The two friends' conversation becomes a veritable seminar on the art of pleasing, a lecture on seduction. In our genealogy, Versac could be seen as the *theoretical* version of Marivaux's Count d'Orsan. The spectacle of gallantry put on by Jacob's friend discreetly acts out an interiorized knowledge of seduction. It has the advantage of aristocratic subtlety and understatement. Although Orsan orders Jacob to imitate him, he does not recite the codes of worldly Society; he limits himself to providing an example, performing a purely spectacular mediation.

Beyond his instruction in the social code, Versac's doctrine can be summarized as a flimsy calculation, a recipe for imitation and singularity. Meilcour remarks on this apparent contradiction in Versac's art, but his initiator clarifies the point immediately: Versac's divine self-sufficiency is only the successful facade of a ruse. The count is an intelligent composite of others: "he added a new charm to everything he repeated" (68), Meilcour himself remarks. The trick is to imitate others, but to send them back an image of themselves that has been rearranged, refashioned by the subject-imitator's intelligence: "a superior genius can enhance what others suggest to him and make it look new even to them" (164). The key to the seducer's entire strategy is in this reflexive or specular artifice. It is a matter of holding up to others the idealized image of themselves, to use the formula I have associated with narcissism. This mimetic perversion is the only way the seducer can become the model of others' desire: " 'Let us sometimes,' says Versac, 'appear their imitators . . . let us help them by our example, and even by our praises' " (163). The seducer calculates ways of abandoning others to the mimetic dynamics of the group, but he does so the better to take his place as their model. He thus feigns peculiarity, the sort of negative, hypocritical mimetic process that Crébillon's text expresses so well: "One cannot therefore be too singular. . . . A folly peculiar to yourself gains you more credit than a virtue shared with another" (162).

But the power of foppery lies less in this art of pleasing—a compromising, coded art, threatened by banality (through rival imitators)—than it does in what Kierkegaard would have called the *intensity* of the practice. This is the sense Versac has in mind, in any case, when he proclaims the genius and the *distinction* of his art: "For whatever the advantages of conceit, it must not be supposed that it can succeed on its own, or that a man who is a fop by nature and not on principle will go as far as one who can exploit his foppishness *with the aid of his reason*, and who, though devoted to the effort to win people over [*de séduire*] . . . is not made drunk by success, and never forgets how to see himself clearly in private" (166; emphasis added).[10]

This scene in Meilcour's initiating process casts Versac as a veritable sorcerer. The secret he hands over to his disciple is in itself a dangerous threat: "if I asked you to keep all that I said absolutely secret, it is because it is of the utmost importance that no one should know what I am and how much I disguise myself" (173).[11] What we must see, then, in the advice that Versac gives Meilcour at the end of the conversation is a kind of impossible challenge, profoundly marked by the *double bind*: "I recommend you, once more, to imitate me" (173). The diabolical nature of Versac's commandment is betrayed in his arrogant, pseudo-divine posture, because the seducer is proposing himself as an inaccessible model. How, in fact, can one trap a person who traps you with his gaze, the gaze of the other—who, with the facility of a magician, undoes what he receives from the other, to the point that this other, blinded, no longer recognizes what comes back to him? How indeed—even if one possesses his ultimate secret—can one imitate the ultimate imitator?[12]

Versac's talent as a seducer nevertheless stumbles up against one character in the novel: Hortense. Representing woman's absolute self-sufficiency and sybilline denial, Hortense reigns over Meilcour's heart like the very sign or hieroglyph of femininity. Standing outside the exchange network, she can only be dreamt about, phantasized. Versac's best weapons are powerless when it comes to her. Hortense functions as Meilcour's excuse, his alibi, in the face of his pseudo-maternal attachment to Madame de Lursay. He will always be able to convince himself that he desires another woman—all the while continuing to fall into the arms of his mother's close friend. At the end of the novel, Meilcour speaks about the "idea" of Hortense. We must take the word *idea* in its strongest sense, that of abstraction or ideality. Unattainable through a series of departures and missed assignations, Hortense will always be absent from the place where Meilcour awaits her. But above all, at the end of the novel, Meilcour undergoes this final frustration: "There were a large number of people at Madame de Lursay's, but I could not see Hortense" (175).

The only possibility left to Meilcour is to return to Madame de Lursay. In order to seduce him this time, she has prepared a ploy that will drive him wild: to arouse Meilcour's desire, it was necessary to find a rival for him. This is the go-between role played by the Marquis de *** at the end of the intricate dance of *The Wayward Head*. Meilcour cannot bear his jealousy: "Such more or less was my situation. I was insensibly yielding to Madame de Lursay without knowing what I was doing. I was outraged that she could think so soon of another engagement, and that which, if I had been able to judge rightly, would have detached me from her for ever, only served to make her more dangerous to my heart than before" (179–80).

This is followed by an even more precise description of mimetic functioning: "She . . . arranged matter so that it was the Marquis, whom I still regarded as my successor, who sat down in the place where I wanted to be. . . . If she had offered the place to me I should certainly not have taken it; but I could not see it filled by another without anger" (181).[13]

This "beguiling coquetry" (181), as Meilcour calls it, will successfully bring about the event so profoundly desired throughout the novel. In spite of the voluptuousness of the "moment," Meilcour is reduced to an almost incestuous sense of guilt. The respect we have mentioned as the interiorization of a filial attitude toward women comes back to tyrannize the young seducer: "The respect she had inspired in me was like those illusions of infancy that one must struggle against so long before they are shattered" (176). What the two lovers seem intent on promising each other is tenderness, a manifestation of an infantile relation (with the combination of nascent eroticism that accompanies it). Meilcour proclaims: "my love [*tendresse*] will leave you nothing to wish for" (198); and Madame de Lursay replies in kind: "I shall feel something not much less than the tenderest love for you" (198).

The curtain falls on the final torment of the hero riven

between fidelity to his mother's friend and his imaginary dealings with Hortense. All that Meilcour can find within himself in his anguish is this fragile contradiction: "Torn away from pleasure by remorse, snatched from remorse by pleasure, I could not be sure of myself for a moment" (201–202).

Part 3

Diabolos

The Power of Evil

Laclos, *Les Liaisons dangereuses*

It was Baudelaire who made it possible to rehabilitate *Les Liaisons dangereuses* by recognizing the tragic dimension of the text, the full extent of its "power of evil."[1] Baudelaire provides the most audacious and accurate analysis of Laclos's novel: he sees *Les Liaisons* as a history book that sheds light on the morals and manners that led up to the Revolution. According to him, it is a "book of sociability"—a terrifying one, he says, its jocular tone notwithstanding. Unfortunately, the book has been reduced to a series of narrative strategies; it has been judged the most brilliantly successful composition, the most effective epistolary novel. The social crisis is conveniently forgotten, and along with it, this portrait of the twilight of the Enlightenment, this historical memoir that Baudelaire so clearly perceived.

Les Liaisons is constructed according to a complex schema of relations. In this study, I will follow only the most important seductions, leaving aside, for example, the relations between Cécile and Danceny, which have a minimal bearing on the text. The perversity of their relationship emerges only in relation to the generalized corruption of the whole. Cécile, in Baudelaire's opinion, is a classic instance of the sensual simpleton, a young woman who needs to be tutored or schooled: her seduction takes on the contours of a sexual education (a bodily apprenticeship under the tutelage of Madame de Merteuil and Valmont) and an education in letters (in more than one sense:

Madame de Merteuil suggests certain readings to Cécile and corrects her epistolary style). In the garden of *Liaisons* where libertines grow, Cécile will soon begin to blossom. . . .

Confining myself, then, to two seducers in the novel—Valmont and Merteuil—I will trace the arabesques and pirouettes of their seductions.

Valmont's career takes a heretofore untrodden path. Familiar with the facile multiplicity of libertine traffic, he has robbed many a sweet young thing of her innocence. He is now in a position to count his conquests, to contemplate his catalog. But one last urge, one last spark of desire piques him: "You know the Présidente de Tourvel: you know her piety, her conjugal devotion, her austere principles. That is where I have launched my attack. There is an enemy worthy of me. That is the goal I aspire to attain" (28–29).[2] The egotistic mission that Valmont proposes will eventually absorb him entirely, to the point that he will end up renouncing altogether the game of libertinage.

What would seem at the beginning to be a trivial choice—Madame de Merteuil, his collaborator, calls it "yet another *rouerie* to include in your memoirs" (21)—shows itself to be the essence of seductive desire: what the seducer desires is to be the other's God, to occupy the very locus of the other's desire. What is at stake in the war between Madame de Merteuil and Valmont is access to this enviable place. These are the terms in which we must understand Valmont's strategy, such as he presents it to his collaborator:

> Conquest is our destiny: we must follow it. Perhaps at the end of the course we shall meet again, for, if I may say this without offending you, my dear Marquise, you follow close at my heels: indeed, it seems to me that our mission of love, since we decided to separate for the general good and have been preaching the faith in our respective spheres, you have made more conversions than I. I know your zeal, your fiery fervour. And if our God judges us by our deeds, you will one day be the patron of some great city, while I shall be, at most, a village saint. (28)

To become the object of the Présidente's devotion is to face long odds indeed: Valmont's target is no less than the locus of absolute desire. In religious devotion, the ultimate form of desire, the subject is entirely appropriated by the object of his passion. To bask in the possession of this desire is certainly the most extreme *jouissance* a seducer can imagine. The Marquise de Merteuil is mistaken when, out of jealousy, she belittles Valmont's object of conquest. The rival to be contended with is not the Présidente's husband, who is absent and powerless; Valmont's attack is aimed not at Madame de Tourvel's fidelity but, rather, at her devotion itself, her passion—what she calls her God. The Présidente's gentle prudishness conceals exactly what Merteuil thinks she lacks: "That absolute self-abandon, that ecstasy of the senses, when pleasure is purified in its own excess" (31). Could it be that even Valmont will stand amazed before this excess? In fact, he observes, the Présidente's fidelity can be explained only as desire maintained at a certain pitch, not as a habit of the senses or as a sterile lack of passion. Devotion only *seems* to be glacial and stony (Madame de Tourvel is "cold and lifeless," 33); in reality it conceals an interior warmth that craves the worship of absent things. Maintaining the presence of such objects—whether God or husband makes little difference—requires a total absorption in phantasm, an extraordinary imaginative capacity: "What an astonishing sensibility she must have, if her feelings extend even to her husband, if she can continue to love a man whom she never sees!" (33).

The target of Valmont's conquest is this quality of desire, the permanent state of phantasy sustained by Madame de Tourvel: "Far be it from me to destroy the prejudices that possess her" (33). The Présidente will maintain this total absorption in phantasy right up until the moment of her collapse. This absorption is what the seducer seeks to divert, to refract in the blinding mirror of his passion: "I shall have this woman. I shall free her from a husband who profanes her. I shall carry her off from the very God that she adores. . . . And I shall indeed be the god of her choice" (33–34). This exquisite instant of egotistic exaltation is worth the wait and the reckless dare. The seducer, crouched like an animal before its prey, has concocted a Mass of his own for the occasion.

From this moment on, the hypocrite-seducer begins to play at God, to ape pious devotion. Not only does he mimic Madame de Tourvel's religious sentiments ("how edified she is by my regular attendance at prayers and at Mass," 29) in order to have her; he even occupies the place of worship. Valmont operates like a veritable sorcerer, a high priest of profanity. Impersonating a man of charity by finding, through his confidant, an unfortunate family in need of help, Valmont arranges for his "natural" compassion to be displayed in front of a large crowd, as if it were entirely unplanned. But the scene evinces all the blasphemous effects of idolatry. The strategy involves ensnaring Madame de Tourvel in her own imagistic trap, making her the spectator to a form of worship that is second nature to her, encouraging the same reverence from her. Valmont places himself exactly in the locus where this image shines most brightly:

> Now I arrive at the village. There is a hubbub. I come forward; I ask questions. I am acquainted with the facts. I summon the tax-collector, and yielding to my generous compassion pay him fifty-six *livres*, for the lack of which sum five persons were to be reduced to living on straw and despair. You cannot imagine the shower of blessings this simple little action brought down upon me from those present, the tears of gratitude that flowed from the eyes of the old paterfamilias, the softening of that patriarchal countenance which only a moment before had been disfigured by a wild and hideous despair. While I contemplated the spectacle, another peasant, a younger man, leading a woman and two children by the hand, rushed towards me and said: "Let us fall at the feet of this image of God," and in an instant the family were on their knees around me. I shall confess to some weakness. My eyes were moist with tears and I felt within me an unwonted but delicious emotion. I was astonished at the pleasure to be derived from doing good, and I am now tempted to think that what we call virtuous people have less claim to

> merit than we are led to believe. Be that as it may, I thought it common justice to repay these poor people for the pleasure they had given me, and I gave them ten *louis* I happened to have on me. Whereupon there was more giving of thanks, but without the same pathos. Necessity had produced the sublime, the true effect. The rest was merely a simple expression of surprise and gratitude for superfluous gifts. (58)

This scene of profanation is worked up into unadulterated narcissistic flattery of the hero. The corruption of Valmont's hypocritical act of charity—"the pleasure to be derived from doing good"—turns out to be "the pleasure they had given me," showing how Valmont manages to place himself at the center of a collective desire. In this sense, he already assumes the figure of the politician creating unanimity in the community. At the center of this idolatry, the seducer feels the warmest narcissistic pleasure. He experiences a painful reflection on his own tableau ("My eyes were moist with tears"). The displeasure that follows the vanishing of this divine instant, this ephemeral brush with transcendence, is understandable. When Valmont passes from an image of God to "the hero in the last act of a drama" (58), he returns to the original emptiness of his desire.

If this satanic pleasure in imitating a god affords Valmont only a brief instant of delight, the effect on Madame de Tourvel could not have been more successful—even though Valmont does not cover up his strategem. Indeed, he confesses his mimetic talent, his play-acting: "Living amongst people without morals, I imitated their vices; perhaps I took pride, too, in outdoing them. Impressed in the same way here by your virtuous example, I have, without hope of emulating it, tried at least to follow it" (62). Despite Valmont's avowal, Madame de Tourvel insists on denying any machinations on his part. She is quite sure his actions are justified by the best of intentions: "there is no question here of a mere fugitive pity . . . but of the solicitude of true charity, of a calculated plan for doing good, of rare virtue in a fine soul" (60). The ploy that Valmont adopts is characteristic of his kind: the seducer is a hypocrite, a mimic, a copier to the core. As with Versac in *The Wayward Head*, the seducer's narcissism only refines or idealizes what he receives from others. If Valmont's scene of pious profanation succeeds, if he makes himself the object of worship, it is by fleshing out an abstract adoration, allowing passion to actualize itself by miming its imaginary appeal.

She-Devil

The seducer, being the great impostor that he is, can also play at miming the one who is seduced, at posing as the target (the victim) of seduction. In order to sensitize Madame de Tourvel to the seduction, Valmont makes her participate in the act of seduction in spite of herself; he elicits feelings in her that were previously completely unknown to her or fearfully repressed. To accuse someone of seductive actions is already to be trapped by the seduction, already to recognize its darkest, most painful signs within the one seduced. The very act of resisting seduction ineluctably requires the one seduced to abandon her innocent passivity. Valmont succeeds in bringing about this complicity by forcing Madame de Tourvel to bear responsibility for the seduction, by reversing their positions as model and object of desire, thus blurring the active and passive roles. Valmont protests that "the extraordinary spell you cast over me makes you absolute mistress of my feelings, and if my love alone is recalcitrant, if that alone you cannot destroy, it is because my love is your own handiwork and not mine" (84). He turns the tables on his partner's accusations: "My whole life is spent in the cruel condition to which you have reduced me, the days in concealing my torments, the nights in suffering them: whereas you live in peace and quiet with no thought of torture but to cause it and commend yourself for doing so. It is you, all the same, who make the accusations, I the excuses" (87).

The seducer, seeking an equal distribution of evil, goes so far as to accuse his target of using deception or devilry: Valmont deplores Madame de Tourvel's "diabolical malice"

(93); she is a "she-devil" (93), he says. The seducer catches his partner failing to live up to her avowed ideal. Thus, for example, Valmont insists on reciprocity as a legitimate demand on Madame de Tourvel's charity: "She refuses to give alms of any kind in the name of love. Being refused them, it seems to me, is more than enough to justify stealing them" (99).

Although Madame de Tourvel defines herself as an anticoquette, adopting an antimimetic stance, she is unaware of just how much her desire to define herself as different from other women—a rebel against a backdrop of sameness—makes her all the more seductive. Her denial only adds to her vanity; she knows herself too well to remain so exceptionally indifferent: "I have none of that vanity which is the reproach of my sex, still less of that false modesty which is only a refinement of pride, and it is in all honesty that I tell you here that I am very little versed in the arts of pleasing" (114). Valmont's grievances against Madame de Tourvel focus on the victim's narcissism, on the self-importance of her proudly displayed modesty: "You pretend to be afraid of love, and do not wish to see that it is you alone who are the cause of the evils for which you hold love to blame" (118); "you should find it more natural to complain of than be surprised at the feelings you inspire" (147). The Présidente is trapped by her own defenses. By the time she asks Valmont, in a last attempt to circumvent the seduction, to limit their relation to pure friendship—that sublimated and desexualized form of passion—it is already too late.

Valmont becomes Madame de Tourvel's *fascinum*, successfully invading the empty space formerly occupied by the imaginary divinity she worshipped. The Présidente's particular psychology is characterized by her imaginative capacity, as we have seen, so that she ends up encountering her object of passion precisely when she is separated from it; it is by absenting himself, by creating the distance of an image, that Valmont is in fact able to accomplish his seduction, to return in triumph to claim Madame de Tourvel. The uncanny problem with distancing oneself is that it creates another trap: a negative coincidence with the object. In the places where Madame de Tourvel goes precisely to find solitude, she discovers the shadow of her seducer following close on her feverish footsteps: "In a few moments I shall have left him and made him unhappy. When he thinks he is still near me, I shall already be far away from him: the hour when I was used to seeing him every day will find me in a place to which he has never been, and where I must never allow him to come" (241).

Inhabited by Valmont's image, the Présidente is no longer able to escape. Valmont has become her phantom, her symptom. As her *fascinum* he exists in the inescapable locus of her desire. He is her fetish, her idol, her divinity: "Fervent prayer, humble supplication, all that mortal man in his terror offers the Divinity, I receive from her" (220). Valmont's name alone has the hallucinatory power to conjure up his presence; hence, his fetishized letters, placed on the altar of love. Madame de Tourvel attributes a sort of occult power to them: "I never opened the letters, but the sight of them would make me weep" (275).

Valmont is the Présidente's poison, her diabolical parasite. At the beginning Madame de Merteuil is rightfully apprehensive about her rival's "fear of the Devil." The Présidente's illness manifests itself as convulsive hysteria; to all intents and purposes, she is possessed.[3] The news of Valmont's death thus comes as deliverance, exorcism, the recovery of reason (allowing her to die): "no sooner had . . . the doctor begun to tell me of the sad accident of Monsieur de Valmont's death, when the unfortunate woman recovered consciousness" (373).

Madame de Tourvel's "fall" consists not in a debasement to the rank of the libertine but, rather, in her joining those *superstitious* women of whom Madame de Merteuil speaks, those who confuse love with a lover and who "with their stupid delusions . . . accord that faith and respect to the priest which is due to only the divinity" (181).

With her customary brutality, Merteuil explains how a certain type of woman can fall victim to her own idealizing projection of the seducer and become blinded by this simulation. Her portrayal of Madame de Tourvel's Valmont-Tartuffe describes the woman's avid simulacrum of the priest: "decking out what is often a very inferior dummy in the vestments of a god. But, whoever he is, they have scarcely dressed him up when, taken in by the illusion of their own creating, they fall to adoring him" (247–48). Madame de Tourvel's *fetishism*, the idolatry that leads her to confuse the sign with the thing, is what brings about her downfall. Her relation to objects—the whole slew of fetishistic paraphernalia with which she surrounds Valmont—reveals the Présidente's superstitious outlook: she is a conjuror of despair. The extreme nature of her desire is less a symptom of a painful lack than it is the *essence* of this archaic sedimentation.[4]

To Be Desire

Like the other seductive heroes we have considered, Valmont possesses a peculiar quality: he is both adored and detested at the same time by the community. His reputation is constructed upon this disturbing paradox: "No one respects him, but everybody flatters him" (77). Like Versac in *The Wayward Head*, Valmont is a sort of phallic slipper that is passed around among women ("I was passed, so to speak, from hand to hand by a series of women" [119]). Like Crébillon's hero, Valmont possesses the knowledge of seduction, the exclusive privilege of the "intensive" seducer. But in our genealogy of seducers, we must place Valmont even higher up. Critics are certainly right to see Versac as a timid ancestor of Valmont (according to La Harpe, "M. de Laclos appears to have added onto Versac of *The Wayward Head*"[5]), but only to the extent that Versac can be considered Valmont's superego; and the two seducers illustrate two different modes of desire. The difference is that Valmont does not imitate or outdo the other seducer. He may show jealousy toward Danceny or even Prévan, but for the most part he ignores his rivals, holding himself above these banal rivalries. Seduction itself becomes a selective activity for him. The master-seducer chooses only the most perfect victims.

What he really wants to imitate is the Other—not his peers

or rivals, but Desire itself: this is the ultimate goal, the apex of seduction. Thus arises Valmont's interest in Madame de Tourvel. All he can do in the face of her religious devotion is to simulate God, become His rival. Valmont's end should be interpreted as a fall not into the banality of possessive love, into fidelity—what a disgrace for a libertine!—but, rather, from the high-stakes game he had set up. Becoming subject and object of the adoration he had prepared for the Présidente, he allows himself to be bewitched by her inflamed spectacle of pleasure, the pious icon of her divine ecstasy. Like a mirror image, Madame de Tourvel has become, in her turn, Valmont's *fascinum*. The Présidente's "fall" through his successful seduction throws back to the seducer's contemplating gaze his victorious narcissism, the specular frenzy of his long-awaited triumph, his coveted complement. The scene in which Madame de Tourvel succumbs is interesting from this point of view: in the annulment of her will, in her annihilation, she becomes a statue, an erect projection of her seducer ("stiff immobility," "fixed expression" [302]). The disappointment that Valmont confesses to Danceny feeds less on the loss of love than on the vanishing shimmer of seduction, transformed in the instant of a sigh into omnipotence, into divinity.

I Have Created Myself

The coquette is subject to the same sort of finality, the same desire for divinity; but in Madame de Merteuil it takes a very different form from Valmont's. The Marquise's libertine culmination lies in the pride of knowledge. In place of coquettish ostentation, she substitutes her principles and her satanic self-sufficiency: "I say '*my* principles' intentionally. They are not, like those of other women, found by chance, accepted unthinkingly, and followed out of habit. They are the fruit of profound reflection. I have created them: I might say that I have created myself" (181).

Creation ("my principles") and self-creation constitute the two aspects of the Marquise's self-sufficiency. If she maintains a kind of personal plurality ("her name is Legion"), it is the better to achieve her satanic solitude: "it amused me to assume different disguises. . . . From that moment on my thoughts were purely for my own benefit" (182). Madame de Merteuil differs from the usual coquette (such as the ones we meet in Marivaux and Crébillon) in her approach to the practice of libertinage. Whereas the common coquette's rejection of men translates into a playful exchange among women that undermines phallic legitimacy, reducing it to a mere commodity devalued by exchange and use, the Marquise perfects this degradation to the point of utter castration. She is an expert in using irony to diminish the possessor of the phallus. Merteuil traps the seducer by flashing his phallic mirage back at him. Her seductive skill always leads to a missed opportunity, a phallic slip, a pitiable *lapsus* on the part of the seducer. The bait she holds out explodes just when it is about to entrap.

This context is what gives Madame de Merteuil's "ambush" of Prévan its significance. The Marquise engineers a seduction—but one that is meant to fail. Faced with the shimmering veil of the desired object, the subject of seduction will remain flabbergasted, disconcerted, embarrassed by his phallic accoutrements:

> Can you see me, Vicomte, in my simple negligee, approaching with timid and circumspect tread, opening the door with an uncertain hand to my conqueror? He saw me. Lightning could not have struck quicker. What more shall I tell you? I was vanquished, utterly vanquished, before I had been able to say a word to stop him or to defend myself. He wanted us next to dispose ourselves more comfortably, and more suitably to the circumstances. He cursed his clothes, which, he said, put him at a disadvantage. He wanted us to fight on equal terms. But my extreme timidity opposed the project, and tender caresses left him no time to carry it out. He occupied himself with other things.
>
> Possessed now of twice his former rights, he revived his claims. . . . As I spoke I rang as hard as I could. Now it was I who had the advantage, and my action was more effective than

> anything he could say. He had done no more than stammer before I heard Victoire come running, calling to the servants she had kept with her as I had commanded. At this point, raising my voice, and in my most regal tone I continued: "You will leave, Monsieur, and never appear in my presence again." At which a crowd of my servants entered the room. Poor Prévan lost his head, and suspecting an ambush in what was at bottom no more than a joke, resorted to his sword—unfortunately for him, since my brave and vigorous *valet de chambre* seized him bodily and threw him to the floor. (203)

Merteuil's three rejections of Valmont's advances later in the novel repeat this same castrating move. What more revealing allusion than for her Merteuil to consider herself "a latter-day Delilah" (186): "Oh, I have my scissors to the hair of a great many of our modern Samsons!" (186). We are far removed from the charms of Marivaux's coquette, her frivolous banter, her unconscious seductions, her art of pleasing that is so full of bad faith. In Madame de Merteuil's case, the die is cast, with the backing of the most powerful will-to-*jouissance* and of the cruelest knowledge. This castrating humor, this supreme posture of self-sufficiency has a name—Pleasure: "Do you know, Vicomte, why I never married again? It was certainly not for lack of advantageous matches: it was solely so that no one should have the right to object to anything I might do. . . . In short, I wished to lie only when I wanted to, not when I had to" (355).

Gonads

Motivated by the same aim—conquest—Valmont and Merteuil attempt to control the fate of others. Seeking to become gods, they end up as demons. In the mirror of their libertinage, in the aura of their false sufficiency, each becomes the other's model or rival. Their competitive relation is what Roland Barthes, with his usual aptness of expression, will call a *correspondence*, "a tactical enterprise to defend positions, make conquests."[6]

Although at the beginning of *Les Liaisons* the Vicomte and the Marquise—surveying the route that stretches out before them and reckoning their paces, nearly in step with each other—optimistically believe their itineraries will converge, we know that this expectation will not be met. If the seducer's mission is to separate (the notion at the etymological origin of the term *seducere*), it must be observed that the separation Valmont and Merteuil undertake is in fact between themselves. The final words of their correspondence ("Very well: war" [358]) signifies this satanic separation.

The epistolary metaphor clarifies the diabolical nature of the system. The key is to hide everything from others and, in so doing, to master their destiny. Valmont and Merteuil have appropriated the divine privilege of *reading the hearts and minds of others*, which becomes a frequent element in the novel. Opened letters, interceptions, and traded stories create a network of misunderstandings. The two interceptors are perverse mediators, parasites,[7] causing static interference in communication and interposing obstacles to the desires of others. Theirs is a perverse monadology.[8] Confined to their misrecognition, the monad-characters are trapped in circuits of deception. The ending of *Les Liaisons* comes as a veritable breakdown of communication provoked by mimetic activity: each character, trying to second-guess the other, attempts to foresee the next blow before it strikes. This game, this pervasive duel, is what Baudrillard sees as the essence of seduction in *Les Liaisons*: "Where there is seduction is not in the relation between seducer and victim, but in that between the seducers, de Valmont and Merteuil, who share a criminal conspiracy by interposed victims."[9]

In his celebrated preface to Laclos's novel, Malraux keenly perceived how imitation—or, better, double imitation—constituted the very basis of the novel; however, he underestimated the full extent of its ineluctable power: "Laclos's characters . . . are all the more drawn to imitation for being themselves the imitators of their own characters."[10] We know how this party ends: the liaisons take a deadly turn. To be precise: Valmont and Madame de Tourvel die; Danceny and Cécile withdraw from the world. But Madame de Merteuil is the one who best articulates the crisis and its resolution and makes manifest the scandal of *Les Liaisons*. The ending of the novel is nothing less than a sacrificial crisis. It must be read not as a hasty resolution to a text that has exhausted its own complications but, rather, as a veritable ritual of execution. The undifferentiated murmuring of the community is heard. Everything is prepared to welcome the victim. Her site is marked out; she rushes towards it, fooled by her executioners' silence:

> Madame de Merteuil, returning from the country the day before yesterday, that is, Thursday, had herself set down at the Comédie Italienne where she had a box. She was alone in it, and, what must have seemed extraordinary to her, not a single man presented himself to her during the entire performance. When it was over, she proceeded, as she usually does, into the small salon, which was already full of people. A murmur immediately went around, of which, however, she apparently did not suppose herself to be the object. She saw an empty place on one of the benches and sat down; whereupon the other women already sitting there rose immediately, as of one accord, and left her absolutely alone. This very marked display of indignation was applauded by all the men, and the hubbub increased to the extent, it is said, of hooting.
>
> So that nothing should be wanting to her humilation, it was her ill fortune that Monsieur de Prévan, who has been seen nowhere since his adventure, entered the same salon at that very moment. As soon as he was seen, everyone, men and women alike, gathered round him and applauded him. He found himself, so to speak, carried before Madame de Merteuil by the company, who then made a circle round them both. The latter, I am assured, maintained an air of neither seeing nor hearing anything, and did not so much as change her expression! But I think this is exaggerated. However that may be, this scene—a truly ignominious one for her—lasted until her carriage was announced. As she left, the *scandalous* jeering was redoubled. (389; emphasis added)

The Marquise de Merteuil becomes the *skandalon*, the one who is blamed for the collective contamination. The purification of the community will be carried out on her body. Laclos's text tries to hide the violence of the mob, in spite of its deafening clamor, by transferring it to the character, by designating it as coming from within the victim: "Madame de Merteuil was attacked the following night by a very violent fever, which, it was thought at first, must be the effect of the terrible predicament in which she had found herself; but since last night it has become known that confluent smallpox of a particularly malignant type has declared itself" (389).[11]

All that remains is to expel the contaminated victim, to chase her from the henceforth purified World: "though she was still ill, she made her arrangements and left during the night by herself taking the post-coach. Her servants said today that none of them wished to go with her. It is thought that she has taken the road for Holland" (392). The contamination now lodges in Merteuil's satanic gaze, which sought to pry into the secrets of others' hearts: "She has recovered, it is true, but horribly disfigured; more than anything by the loss of an eye. . . . I am told that she looks truly hideous" (392).[12] This face, permanently marked by the evil that had previously lurked within, now shows its dark underside: "the disease has turned her inside out . . . her soul is now visible on her face" (392). The ugliness of her frightful features makes her instantly recognizable as the dreaded Gorgon. The punishment that strikes Madame de Merteuil is Laclos's terrifying representation of her vengeful and guilty sexuality. What she is condemned to display in this perfectly figural eye is the monstrosity of her genitalia.[13]

Beasts

Heiner Müller's *Quartet*, an adaptation of *Les Liaisons dangereuses*, places its characters in a virtual hell.[14] Eliminating all but Valmont and Merteuil, the playwright opposes these two to one another in a diabolical symmetry, as in a mirror. Müller carries their resemblance so far as to make each speak in the other's place, thus inverting their roles. The other characters of the infernal quartet are summoned to appear solely through the syntax of slander. Thus the Présidente de Tourvel is cut down in a few ignominious words: "that cow . . . a mighty lump of flesh . . . left-overs" whose "hands will not touch any genitals . . . without the blessing of the church" (4–5). Cécile Volanges is no more than a wretched metonymic effect, reduced to her "virginal bottom" and her "pink instrument" (10). From Laclos's erotic libertinage, Müller has distilled the bestiality of hate and the perversity of desire. He has placed the characters in an atmosphere of decomposition that redoubles their internal taint. This is where the war between Valmont and Merteuil takes place, with knives drawn and teeth bared: a fight to the finish. In this sense, Müller's adaptation can be seen not only as one of the most provocative but also as one of the most faithful readings of Laclos. *Quartet* is the theater of disillusioned, defunct flesh. Laclos's boudoir has become a bastion of decay. The mirrors no longer reflect elegant lines, affected masks; quite the contrary, they expose their defaced silvering, their damaged surface: they "sweat out . . . blood" (7).

The author understood that for these two seducers the aim of seduction was to forget slavish mundanity; their sole preoccupation was to envy divinity. Merteuil laments the "torment of living and not being God" (3). Müller's drama endows this character in particular with an icy self-sufficiency. In the *Liaisons*, Merteuil was a sort of Minerva whose seduction seemed to spring forth from her brain: she appeared to have transplanted her sexual organ to her head. In Müller's play, she becomes a ferocious statue, a purely evil brain: "What do I care for the lust of my body, I am not a milkmaid. My brain is functioning normally. I am quite cold, Valmont" (3).

Merteuil's castrating dream in *Quartet* is a statuary dream. Her gaze is as cold as death. If in the *Liaisons* she ends up as the Gorgon, here her innermost desire is to be the Medusa, to possess the other with her terrifying eye: "provided that I could now turn you to stone with the loving glance of Medusa. . . . We'd have full houses, don't you think, Valmont, with the statues of our decayed desires" (4). Escaping the public condemnation that she suffers in the novel, the Merteuil of Müller's play punishes herself: she speaks of mutilating her genitals to keep them permanently out of the reach of her past lover. A venomous Venus, she proclaims herself utterly whored, and Valmont joins her in a gesture of mutual poisoning.

Quartet transforms the boudoir of the *Liaisons* into an infernal bunker. As reread by Müller, Laclos is tinged with Sade. Or rather, Müller confers on the text of the *Liaisons* the scope of decay and bestiality that Laclos's libertinage had spared it: his epistolary detour avoided the actual confrontation of doubles, the inexorable devouring logic. Facing his diabolical partner, Valmont refers to their roles as "the theatricality of beasts" (7). The play ends in an atmosphere of putrid reciprocity, the characters succumbing to the gangrene of Evil. They shout each other's heads off in the moments before death, in their wish for the terminal catastrophe, the spectacular pestilential orgy. To desire one another, they had offered each other their cruellest abomination: "we are alone Cancer my loved one" (16).

Gonadology

Sade, *Juliette*

Il faut toujours en revenir à Sade
pour expliquer le mal.[1]
—BAUDELAIRE

Leaving the *Liaisons*, we might usefully ponder the state of relations in Sade. The Sadean novel celebrates liaisons *in extremis*, tracing their complex nexus to its breaking point. Sade's system is bent on denying relations, but to do so, it constantly posits them, probing their foundation: the Sadean text is eminently anthropological, in that it constantly posits the nature (the "naturalness") of every kind of relation from every possible angle (sexual, familial, societal). It thus represents the logical endpoint of this book, which has attempted, starting from Marivaux, to investigate this problem by undertaking a sort of anthropology of the eighteenth-century novel.

Poised at the twilight of the Enlightenment, Sade is a clamorous harbinger of the nineteenth century. Baudelaire is his closest cousin, his first true echo. Sade is no anomaly of the Enlightenment. All he did, as a good reader and anthropologist of his century, was to expand on the terror of relations we have already seen outlined in the texts discussed thus far. In retrospect, Sade can be seen to represent a logical outcome—but of a process already corrupt. All that was necessary was to rip off the veil, to reveal the formulae concealed beneath layers of makeup, to unmask the bewigged monsters, and expose to the blinding light of day the depths of evil hidden under the cover of libertinage.

Sade also represents the twilight of adornments and finery. No longer mysterious beings hiding behind their masks and veils, Sade's figures are walking mirrors of their souls. The Sadean being immediately lets his nudity be seen: it is his only adornment—waist, breast, buttocks, cunt, prick, ass. . . . Modesty plays no part in this spectacle of the body. The whole structure of respect that restrained characters in earlier novels has vanished. In the words of Sade's character Delbène, "Modesty is an illusion—resulting from what? 'tis the result of nought but our cultural manners and our upbringing, it is what is known as a conventional habit. Nature having created man and woman naked, it is unthinkable that she could have implanted in them an aversion or a shame thus to appear" (5).[2] Juliette is quick to tell Clairwil: "Let's be rid of these inopportune raiments" (275). Clothing is an obstacle to immediate possession. It postpones the moment of lustful concupiscence, interposes an imaginary dimension of desire, uselessly mediates seduction: "lewd debauch calls for nakedness" (275). The Sadean project is to see into the deepest recesses of the other, to bask in the transparency of evil: "I've not the faintest idea how you are made, I wish to see everything . . . ah, I want to see your heart throb, your breast quiver from the excitement I cause in you" (275). As Philippe Roger writes: "Nudity is not a value in Sade (as it does in contemporary eroticism); it represents the state required for the body's most complete availability."[3]

What sent Sade to prison was not only the horror of his writing; it was his unblinking, blinding look at a century that used Reason as a reassuring mask for its fears, as a voice for its silence, as a light for its shadows.[4] Sade's text is the blueprint, the graph, the palimpsest of his fearful century. We shall see just how apt was Michel Foucault's presentation of Sade's "impossible" text as "an obvious pastiche of all the philosophies and narratives of the eighteenth century."[5]

In Laclos, Leibniz's monadology is perverted: Valmont and Merteuil fight over the divine monad, the panopticon of seduction. In Sade, this perversion is made even more radical. The principle is simple: "*to enjoy oneself at the expense of no matter whom*" (52). The entire network of relations in Laclos must pass through the couple Merteuil-Valmont. Together they usurp the divine site from which the transparent destiny of others can be viewed. In Sade, each libertine becomes the other's god: this is the profane view of the divinity offered by the dazzling shimmer of Sadean monadology.[6] Saint-Fond says it outright, to Juliette's face: "we are so many gods" (243). He continues: "Ah, is it not obvious that among men, or rather, above men, there is a class so superior to the weaker sort as to be what of old the poets termed divinities?" (243). Philosophical interpretations of Sade, including Blanchot's, arrive at similar conclusions: "Sadean man denies man, and this negation is achieved through the intermediary of the notion of God. He temporarily makes himself God, so that there before him men are reduced to nothing and discover the nothingness of a being before God."[7]

And Klossowski writes: "If Sade at first held to the denial of evil, he is not yet satisfied with this negation. The reason is that the neighbor [*prochain*] is found to be involved; and as long as the neighbor exists for the *ego*, he reveals the presence of God."[8] This diabolical system, this staggering monadology, is best realized through the Sadean orgy, which is based on the principle of *imitation*: its *modus operandi* is to copy, to imagine the other's desire, to outdo the other libertine's imagination. But in appearance, rivalry and sexual competition are effaced. The orgy seeks to effectuate a lack of differentiation, an erotic homogenization of individuals. It is a sort of mimetic utopia. Erotic behaviors are literally *copied*, in an almost animal fashion ("Tell me, what do you desire?"). The etiquette of orgiastic acts is essentially imitative. "Imitate me!" the libertine is constantly crying during scenes of debauchery:

> "you'll soon be imitating me" (Delbène to Juliette, 20);
>
> "we are going to teach you to imitate us" (56);
>
> "I piss; the tureen goes from hand to hand, the whores all drink their fill, the men do the same" (Juliette, 96);

"I would have you imitate your friends, you're to shit as did they." (Mondor to Juliette, 164)

The epic aspects of mimesis are dramatized through the synchronization of bodies, the homogenization of erotic zones, the exhaustive reciprocity of pleasures, the interchangeability of victims, and the utopian search for their multiplicity. Bodies are absolute in their refraction and reversibility. Giving is effaced by asking; the cause (of pleasure) tends to efface the effect. Such is Sade's erotic machine. It is perfectly saturated, and reversible:

Télème, who'd just fucked my cunt, arranged himself in my ass; his device was a shade thicker than his confrere's, but, novice though I was, Nature had apparently so well modeled me for these doings that I confronted an increased diameter with an accommodating elasticity. I was lying flat upon the Superior, in such wise that my clitoris was directly over her mouth, and the gay wench, happily sprawled on the hard stone floor, was sucking like a babe on a teat; her thighs were wideflung. Between them, Laurette, bent over her, was treating her as I was being dealt with and, rocked by pleasure, the lewd thing was frantically masturbating Volmar on one side and Flavie on the other. Behind Laurette, Ducroz was gently frigging his tool on her buttock. (57)

Hither, Juliette, I want to cunt-suck you while our wights embugger me; squatting over your visage, Volmar will present her charms to you, you'll lech them, you'll sup on them while with your right hand you pollute Flavie and with your left you give Laurette's buttocks a smart spanking. (90–91)

All contagious forms of mimesis are to be found in Sade. Epidemics, gangrene, plague: libertinage embraces all these names in its desire for absolute undifferentiation. The Sadean seducer is first and foremost a *schoolteacher*; he needs to command imitation, to convert, to discover in the other the scintillating specularity of evil. Sadean pedagogy is a pure mediation of desire (Sade's work, as is often remarked, is a "school of libertinage"[9]). The Sadean teacher is the model of pleasure. That is why there are no more games in Sadean seduction. The stakes are in a sense too high: "for a libertine intelligence, there is no more piercing pleasure than that of making proselytes. A thrill marks the inculcation of each principle, a multitude of various feelings are flattered by the sight of others becoming gangrened by the very corruption that rots us. Ah, how it is to be cherished, that influence obtained over their souls, souls which are finally re-created by our counsels, urgings, and seductions" (52). Delbène declares: "my libertinage is an epidemic, whosoever is in my vicinity is bound to be infected by it" (12).

Imitation is not simply instinctive or literal. The specular game of the orgy targets not only the other's body, but also his reflection. As Barthes remarked, mirrors have a special place in the Sadean orgy.[10] They bring the specularity of sexual objects to a dazzling focus (this apt mirror metaphor comes straight from Delbène's lips: "the more highly polished the mirror, the better it receives and the better reflects the objects presented it" [54]). Pleasure stems less from the multiplication of the object than it does from its exhaustion, through a radical externalization of desire and the individual. Sadean mirrors abolish the seducer's narcissistic game (whence their multiplication): they expose the falseness of his self-sufficiency. In Dolmancé's boudoir (*Philosophy in the Bedroom*), mirrors reflect not so much an aesthetic device as a theory of desire. The spectacle afforded by the mirrors makes it possible to imitate not the other, but the other's pleasure. The watched, imitated subject disappears behind his pleasure:

> Eugénie: . . . But why all these mirrors?
> Mme de Saint-Ange: By repeating our attitudes and postures in a thousand different ways, they infinitely multiply those same pleasures for the persons seated here upon this ottoman. Thus everything is visible, no part of the body can remain hidden: everything must be seen; these images are so many groups disposed around those enchained by love, *as many delicious tableaux as there are imitators of their pleasures*, wherewith lewdness waxes drunk and which soon serves to complete itself in climax.[11]

We are now in a position to understand what has been called Sadean egoism and to return to the "ethics" it propounds regarding the orgy. The Sadean being, with his desire to be a god for the other, is first of all a separate individual. Noirceuil describes the biological birth of beings thus: "All living creatures are born isolated" (176). The corrupt principle of the gift is most fully realized in the orgy: "I give unto you in order that I may obtain from you in exchange" (144). Delbène also says: "Pray avail me of that part of your body which is capable of giving me a moment's satisfaction, and, if you are so inclined, amuse yourself with whatever part of mine may be agreeable to you" (63–64). In other words, by giving oneself to everyone, one gives oneself first to oneself. This is the perverse equilibrium of the orgy. Rousseau's general will (*volonté générale*) is eroticized, replaced by general lust (*volupté générale*). General lust recognizes no brotherhood: "I haven't the slightest germ of belief in that *bond of fraternity* I hear fools prate about unendingly" (100). A bond or a biological continuity between beings is a mirage: "There is then no kind of real bond between another human being and myself . . . the only manner in which I need act with this other individual is to wrest from him all I possibly can and cede him as little" (Noirceuil [179]). Vice and crime reestablish the link that nature has failed to provide. Libertinage, in the guise of exhaustivity, in its totalitarian gathering of bodies, is a praxis of separation. Permutation, the principle par excellence of the Sadean orgy, is never realized better than through separation. Once again, Delbène pointedly gives expression to this libertine contradiction: "Voluptuousness can tolerate no inhibitions, it attains its zenith only by shattering them all. Now, the stronger a person's intellectual endowments, the more restraints he breaks, and the more decisively: hence, the person of superior wit and parts will always be found more apt to libertinage's pleasures" (53–54).

Libertinage thus desires to satiate all mimetic rivalry, by feigning undifferentiation. The Sodality of the Friends of Crime is founded on this paradoxical principle; it is, in fact, the society's first law: "No distinction is drawn among the individuals who comprise the Sodality; not that it holds all men equal in the eyes of Nature—a vulgar notion deriving from infirmity, want of logic, and false philosophy—but because it is persuaded and maintains that distinctions of any kind may have a detrimental influence upon the Sodality's pleasures" (418). Marriage is excluded from the Sadean system because it represents a sort of anthropological aberration. According to the mimetic principle, marriage withholds an object desired by the other; the monogamous relation is false because it keeps rivals at bay and fosters competition. One might as well return to the neutrality of inconstancy, then, to the bewitching pleasures of debauchery. Noirceuil explains Saint-Fond's rivalrous perversion to Juliette:

> The idea of you lying in another's arms entrances Saint-Fond, he himself puts you there, knowing you there, imagining you there, seeing you there hardens his prick; you'll multiply his pleasures as proportionally you augment the size and number of your own, and Saint-Fond will never cherish you so much as when you do to the utmost that which would earn you the hatred of a clod. (260)

But it is not so clear that this mimetic machine functions so well, after all. The desire for superiority resurfaces at the heart of pleasure and reestablishes differences. There are libertines and then there are Libertines. Noirceuil can thus place himself before Juliette as the absolute, and thus (paradoxically) inimitable, model or, rather, as maintaining the other's permanent desire for imitation: "'I have never beheld a creature more analogous to me; I'd adore her if 'twere in my power to love a woman. . . . Would you imitate me, Juliette? I defy thee to do so. If what were enclosed in my heart could be opened to the light, it would so horrify the race of men there'd perhaps not be one amongst them all who'd dare come within sight of me'" (185). In orgies the most disturbing distance is created by preference: Juliette tells us that "Delbène shortly perceived that I preferred Sainte-Elme to her" (27). Clairwil is actually killed by Durand's intermediary so that Durand will remain Juliette's sole model, her only idol. The constant need for victims also proves that rivalry is never actually appeased. Sacrifices must proliferate. The libertine's mimetic rivalry discharges itself on the body of the victim: in the victim's body the libertine desire for undifferentiation comes to a head and to an end. Marcel Hénaff rightly says that "the victim's body necessarily appears instead of and in the place of the missing mirror,"[12] in that obscure, imaginary place where their desires for domination and superiority collide. In any case, it is only in the context of imitation that Sadean desire, Sade's theory of libertinism, and his system can be understood. His doctrine could be summed up in a phrase from *La Nouvelle Justine*, in which all rivalries are maintained: *imitate, but while hating; copy, but while cursing*.[13]

Idols and Neighbors

Coquettes do not fare well in Sade. They are completely used, *screwed over*. Up until now, coquetry has hidden behind flirting and games, sublimating the horror of using and being used. In Sade, the female libertine meets her exploiter at least halfway. The coquette is first and foremost a whore. Delbène (a sort of mother superior of Arpajon, minus the remorse) cries out in a rush of *jouissance*: "I confess to you that I'm capable of envying the fate of those heavenly creatures who ornament street corners and slake the filthy lust of whoever strolls by" (90). It is not difficult to understand why Sade loved *Manon* and ranked Prévost's heroine above all novelistic creations of his century. In Delbène's words, "A whore is a lovable creature, young, voluptuous, who, less interested in her reputation than in the welfare of others, on those grounds alone merits every praise. The whore is the beloved child of Nature, the abstinent girl is Nature's execration; the whore is deserving of altars, the vestal of the stake" (84–85). To prostitute oneself means to annihilate oneself in the other's filth, to abominate oneself for the sake of the other's desire; it means to idolize the other's desire to the point of desecrating one's own desire. The whore is always sacrificed, a vestal to the other's passion. This externalization of her desire for prostitution in a sense rectifies what happens in Manon's case, in which this desire, excused by financial need, remains discreet and refuses to declare itself. In Sade, the desire for prostitution is pure *jouissance*, a maximization of exchange and use.

The second degraded figure of coquetry is the witch. Unlike Manon, who was able to enchant Des Grieux, or Marivaux's coquettes, who trailed their spellbinding mirrors about with them, Sade's sorceress is no longer a simple, fairy-tale creature phantasized by the fearful imagination of the other. She is real and her powers of fascination are fatal. Her libertinage is infected with the most terrifying strain of evil. The witch represents the exacerbated figure of seduction gone bad, of wicked enchantment. In *Juliette*, this role is played by Durand. Although Manon was accused of being a poison for Des Grieux, her bewitchment remained spiritual and her diabolical charms seemed mysterious to us; they took effect in the distance that opened up between the two characters, in the intersection of their impossible desires. Manon's sybilline persona alone constituted the poison. Her emanation, her scent were diabolical.

Durand's seductions have nothing of this silent charm; they are straightforwardly effective—making use of sundry poisons and the handiest of tools. Appearing in the midst of her stills, ovens, jars, and books, Durand is in her element in an atmosphere of sulphur and amber. A pharmacist of desire, she has at her disposal not only philters and aphrodisiacs ("cantharides, ginseng, and several vials of Joui liqueur from Japan" [532]) but also devices such as the "phantom-phallus" she uses on Clairwil and Juliette: "a prick made contact with our behinds, was rubbed in the blood oozing forth from them; some sighs, some voluptuous moans were heard, and two or three kisses were bestowed on our assholes, a tongue even twittered into them, then twittered out again" (529).

Through her sexual monstrosity—her vagina is "obstructed" (1032 [*barré*])—Durand brings to a head and perverts the coquette's desire for (sexual) self-sufficiency. Castrating and essentially phallic (although her vagina is obstructed, she possesses a rare clitoris: "never had we in all our days seen one so long nor so straight-standing" [534]), she refuses frontal penetration by a man: she insists on the sodomist's inverted, unnatural approach. But this compensation is the source, as we know, of the purest Sadean *jouissance*. At once physicist, chemist, and pharmacist, Durand appears as the apogee of woman in *Juliette*. A rival to God, she knows all the world's secrets:

> I hold the lives of multitudes in my hands: I can send the plague roaring abroad, poison streams and wells, propagate epidemics, contaminate the air of provinces, clap blight on houses, fields, vineyards, murrain on flocks; into deadly poison transform the flesh of cattle, I cause villages to burn, make suddenly perish he who inhales the scent of a flower or who unseals a letter; in a word, I am a woman without peer in my kind, nay, I am unique in it. (540)

As an artist of separation, like the chemist Almani in *La Nouvelle Justine*, Durand is pure evil energy—what Merteuil was unable to become. Yet, in Durand's statement "I am a woman without peer" (spoken in another context to indicate her phallic resistance: "Cunt-fucking is not to my liking" [534]) we recognize the Marquise's "I have created myself." With her knowledge of souls, Durand is able to dispense all desires: " 'There is not a single passion,' replied Durand, 'not a single whim or fancy, not a living being on this globe, not an extravagance or eccentricity, however unusual or picturesque it be, that cannot be enjoyed here' " (542–43).

Such is the coquette's epic career, as conceived by Sade. In his work all the heroines of the eighteenth-century novel appear in a perverted form: for each of them he has a malefic metamorphosis in store. But the most astonishing success of Sade's invention is Juliette's offspring. Her daughter, a child of vice and product of crime, bears the name of the creature known as the most virtuous heroine of all Enlightenment novels: Marianne. In the end, she is murdered by her triumphant mother in a deadly fire. This perverse echo rings out the eighteenth-century novel.

Pandora's Box

Sade's character Saint-Fond takes his place next to Durand as a *ne plus ultra* of the seducer. The reason: his belief in an infernal deity. If Valmont places himself in the locus of pious devotion, playing the hypocrite, Saint-Fond carries the strategy to an extreme. But Saint-Fond, lacking Valmont's hypocritical conscience, perverts worship in order to avoid being caught out at his own game. By treating it ironically, he himself undoes the adoration that he sets up. He is the object of his own blasphemy. The Sadean model, through his own devices, is his own enemy; he suffers from his own destruction. In Sade, the ego-ideal has become sullied, rotten. Noirceuil has his Phallus-God worshipped; Saint-Fond's cult is even crueler: "I had to make a god of his very mard" (236).

One scene in *Juliette* corresponds precisely to Valmont's famous scene of idolatry in *Les Liaisons*. Once again, the scene is arranged by Juliette. Naturally, the effect on the seducer is different, the perverse reversals striking. The seducer's narcissism is not in the least flattered; in fact, he remains quite unmoved. What immediately excites his lascivious desire is the spectacle of his own evil:

> [A]n old beggarwoman accosted us, asking for alms. . . . And catching the Minister by the hand, she guided him into a mean little hut lit by a lamp hung from the ceiling, and where two children, one male and the other female, and no older than eight or ten, were lying naked on some rotten straw.
>
> "Behold this unhappy family," the pauper said to us; "it's been three days since I was able to give them a crust of bread. Have the kindness, you who are reputed so very rich, to give me the wherewithal to sustain my children awhile in their sorry

existence. Oh, my Lord, I know not who you are; but are you acquainted with Monsieur de Saint-Fond?"

"I am," said the Minister.

"Ah then! you see his handiwork before you. He had my husband taken off to jail; he deprived us of the little that we possessed of goods; such are the cruel circumstances we are reduced to since above a year. . . ."

The great thing about this scene, my friends, the thing in which I could take pride, was its complete authenticity: I had unearthed these wretched victims of Saint-Fond's injustice and rapacity, I now presented them to him in the flesh, to reawaken his wickedness.

"Ah, the scoundrel!" exclaimed the Minister, staring fixedly at the humble woman, "yes, I know him well, by God I do, and you shall come to know him too: he stands before you. . . .

Whereupon, his prick prodigiously stiffened by all the foregoing, the wag bends, seizes the little boy, and embuggers him on the spot; next catching hold of the little girl, he does the same with her. Then, very heatedly he cries: "Lousy old bitch, show me your bewrinkled bum, I require the sight of your flapping buttocks in order to unload."

The old woman weeps, she resists; I lend Saint-Fond my aid. Having heaped insults upon that woebegone ass, the libertine penetrates it, while trampling on the brats, literally crushing them beneath his boots as he sodomizes their mother, and at the moment of his discharge he fires a bullet into her brain. And we depart from that den of misfortune. (245–47)

The motivating principle in Saint-Fond's system is to be the other's God. When he asks Juliette to imitate him, it is to teach her this new state of affairs: "But you, Juliette, ah! hurl all Nature into confusion . . . men will consider your anger godlike and do you divine worship . . . and will dread you when in wrath you trample upon it; but it is all one, whatever you do, you'll always be God to the common sort and mass of humankind" (343). In Saint-Fond, the desire for divinity takes the form of despotism, the locus of the "he," the third person—

the phantasmatic presence of God—in which the libertine insists on being addressed. The desire of this infernal monster is first of all destructive, separative. He wants to be a sort of Pandora's box from which all the evils of the world would issue, coming to destroy mortals "piecemeal" (243).

The libertine imposes the law of his desire on the other; the victim recognizes in the libertine the law of his or her own desire. The spectacle of Sadean harems gives an idea of the impossible swath of this tyranny: "I affirm that the fundamental, profoundest, and keenest penchant in man is incontestably to enchain his fellow creatures and to tyrannize them with all his might" (317). Under the gaze of the despot, Juliette comes to reflect on her obedience: "to me you are as a god, 'tis at your feet I want to pass my life" (323). This refraction of divinity, passed from Saint-Fond to Juliette, will be relayed to Clairwil: "You are a god to me," she says to Juliette.

Saint-Fond's black masses, the desecration of the Pope in *Juliette*, the sacrifical ceremonies and erotic rituals contain and elaborate on this rivalry with divinity. Sade's atheism is clear in its principles, but its confirmation through repetition in the libertine discourse necessitates a phantom God. God himself becomes the Phallus: "'What a tale of crimes that prick has cost me!" he cried, "what a host of execrable things have I done in order that it might surrender its sperm a slight shade more hotly. Upon this globe's whole extent there is not a single object I'm not ready to sacrifice to its comfort: this tool is my god, let it be one unto thee, Juliette: extol it, worship it, this despotic engine'" (185).

God appears in this atheistic refutation only to be denied, exhibiting his crude erection (indeed, the libertine is fond of proclaiming the futility of God and the fantastical or monstrous erection of such an idol. For Durand as well, God is confused with her "phantom phallus," which mysteriously penetrates Juliette and Clairwil.

If libertine seduction is to be absolute persuasion, it must eliminate all traces of this chimerical divinity and occupy its place. That is why in Sade's text, libertinage is first of all a seduction of principles that operates by eroticizing philosophical discourse. In *Les Liaisons*, the place Valmont wanted to usurp was that of Desire or passion. In Sade, the place to be usurped is that of every passion, of all the passions that move humankind ("the fires of emotion cindered that odious scare, the Divinity" [88]). The Sadean system wants to occupy the precise locus of this motivation. Religion is the reign of passions (hence the unbridled penchant for superstition); that, therefore, is what must be stolen away from God. The chimera of religion must be replaced by the Chimera of Passions. Imagination thus becomes the libertine's most precious asset. Imagination alone seduces. As Hubert Damisch explains, imagination in Sade's work is far from a compensatory activity (affording deliverance, through fiction or dream, from common social repression); it is called to surpass itself, to exceed its own capacities. It must submit to a "systematic disturbance" that realizes man not such as he is but such as he might be modified by vice, by passions—in short, by crime. In this sense, the effective imagination wishes to be *inconceivable*.[14] Saint-Fond, Durand, Noirceuil, Belmor, and Juliette are first and foremost imaginative beings.

> "This imagination you laud in me, Juliette," [Saint-Fond] said one day, "is precisely what in you seduced me; for lasciviousness, diversity, and energy I have seldom seen its equal; and you have surely remarked that my sweetest pleasures with you are those I taste when, the two of us giving free rein to fancy, we fabricate ideal lubricities whose existence, unfortunately, is impossible. Oh, Juliette, how delicious are the pleasures of the imagination, and how voluptuously one follows out the lines of its dazzling constructions! Ah, dear angel, how little do they realize what we are about, what we originate, what we create during these divine intervals when our fiery souls are plunged utterly into the impure depths of lubricity; what raptures we experience as, frigging each other, we come erect erecting phantoms; nor with what ecstatic joy we caress them . . . elaborate them . . . surround them with a thousand obscene details and episodes. All the earth is ours in these enchanted moments; not a single creature resists us, to our aroused senses each af-

> fords the kind of pleasure which to our boiling imagination each appears capable of giving; we devastate the planet . . . and repeople it with new objects, and immolate these in their turn; the means to every crime is ours, we commit them all; we multiply the horror a hundredfold; and all the deeds ambitioned by all the most infernal and the most malignant spirits that ever were, in their most disastrous effects were nought compared to what we dare desire. . . . "Happy," says La Mettrie, "happy they whose lively and wanton imagination keeps their senses ever whetted to the foretaste of pleasure!" (521–22)

Sade must be restored to his diabolical status. We must recognize his work as the Luciferian spectacle it is and acknowledge these erotic sacrifices as celebrations of a black mass: "Oh Lucifer! You whom I adore" (693) recites Bernis in an orgiastic session in *Juliette*.[15] We must see *Juliette* as something beyond the rational demonization that Adorno and Horkheimer ascribe to the novel in *Dialectic of Enlightenment*:

> [Juliette] demonizes Catholicism as the most up-to-date mythology, and because of this, and with it, civilization as a whole. The energies which were devoted to the Blessed Sacrament, are applied to sacrilege instead. But this reversal is merely attributed to society. . . . The primeval behaviors which civilization had made taboo had led a subterranean existence, having transformed into destructive tendencies under the stigma of bestiality. Juliette practices them not as natural but as tabooed activities. . . . Not unlike Merteuil in the *Liaisons Dangereuses*, Juliette embodies (in psychological terms) neither an unsublimated nor regressive libido, but intellectual pleasure in regression, *amor intellectualis diaboli*, the pleasure of attacking civilization with its own weapons.[16]

Where Adorno and Horkheimer call for a social criticism, a simple perversion, we need to substitute an anthropological restoration of Sade's infernal intention, to revive its fundamental archaism.

Saint-Fond the alchemist, Durand the witch, and Sade the

Freemason all stir up this underside of the Enlightenment, its shadowy nether regions. They lurk in the tombs of the *philosophes* and scatter their deceitful remains. In the infernal trinity of Noirceuil, Juliette, and Durand, the ending of *Juliette* announces the voluptuous institution of a diabolical government, a State of Evil. The three career toward power, armed with Durand's secret—the secret of a fucking God that will never be revealed to us.

Deadly Quadrille

Goethe, *Elective Affinities*

According to the schema of relations examined thus far, *Elective Affinities* is the inverse of *Les Liaisons dangereuses*. Both texts are about communication, about systems of exchange. *Les Liaisons* is modeled, as I have argued, on a perverted monadology. *Elective Affinities*, on the contrary, presents itself from the outset as a harmonious system. Charlotte and Eduard's marriage constitutes a fixed system of successful communication. Hence Charlotte's "superstitious" fear (to use Eduard's term) of introducing an "impediment" or interference into the system, when Eduard wishes to invite his friend, Captain Othon. The text opens with this fear of an intrusive third party, a *parasite* in both senses—static interference and organic invasion: "There is nothing of more significance in any situation than the intervention of a third party. I have known friends, brothers and sisters, lovers, married couples, whose relationship has been altogether changed, whose life has been turned upside down, by the chance or intended arrival of another person" (25).[1] The captain occupies the position of this feared third party in the novel. His presence will, in fact, prove disruptive, disturbing the nature of the couple's relations. From the moment of his arrival, he has a divisive effect. Appropriating Eduard's presence through mimetic attraction, through a desire for twinship, the captain begins by upsetting the sexual economy of the household:

"The men went about their affairs in closer and closer companionship (they were in particular taking great care of the nursery gardens and glasshouses . . .), Charlotte began to feel more and more lonely as the days went by" (42).

Everything in *Elective Affinities* points to the notion that work strengthens ties while sidestepping the terrifying encounter with the relation. The captain's inordinate commitment to work does in fact seem to betray a certain panic: "Few men could manage with as little sleep as he could and he always devoted the day to the task in hand, so that each evening something had been done" (46). The text expresses this mania for productivity extremely well. Everything is oriented toward production. The captain's world is a classified, inventoried world; the entire space is occupied, measured, surveyed, leveled. The captain is an archivist par excellence. His universe is one of representation. The text expresses the old soldier's hysterical or symptomatic *ordering* through the exhaustive, totalizing effect of words: "They installed in the Captain's wing a registry for current documents, an archive for those no longer current. They collected together all the papers and reports which lay scattered in containers, rooms, cupboards and boxes. With the greatest of speed the chaos was reduced to a gratifying order and lay captioned in named compartments" (46–47).

How can the problem of the unwelcome third person be solved? We know what Charlotte suggests to Eduard: to have her niece and foster-daughter, Ottilie, join the household. Her approach is to introduce more interference into the system, to saturate it somehow. Ottilie's presence is meant to neutralize the triangular system, but in actuality she assumes the new role of the third party in relation to the others. The quadrille that they are about to dance provides only the semblance of a solution to the problem. Indeed, the addition of Ottilie will complicate the situation, upsetting the existing network of relations. The chemistry metaphor that originally inspired Goethe works on all levels: a "quadrille" is an example of an affinity, *attractio electiva duplex*.[2] Michel Tournier, in his preface to the French translation of Goethe's novel, points to the origin of the term *quadrille* as traced by J. S. T. Gehler in his *Dictionary of Physics*.

The captain is the third element, but he is also the intermediary, the chemist, the analyst, the "divorcer" (53),[3] the expert in the art of separations and attractions. What we are faced with, then, is a complicated quadrilateral, an intense matrix of mimeticism. The players in this quartet are playing a variation on musical chairs, but it is as if each one is the fifth player, trying in the maddening rush for a partner to occupy the last empty chair, to oust another player rather than be the odd one out. What is striking about Goethe's text is the way these relations are chosen (Charlotte and the Captain/Ottilie and Eduard) under the silent, collusive, compromising gaze of the other partners in the dance: they are silent seductions, scenes not heard. The scenarios of reading and musical performance reveal the intensity of the characters' desire to imitate each other and the degree of the delicate rivalry that exists between them: "'They can do it better than we can, Ottilie!' said Eduard. 'Let us admire them, but let us go on enjoying our own playing too'" (81). Looks and intimate secrets are conspiratorially reflected and exchanged. In order to seduce Eduard, Ottilie imitates his performance from memory: "She had made his shortcomings so much her own that a new living whole had evolved which, if it did not keep to the original measure, at any rate managed to sound very pleasant and agreeable" (80). This resurgence of memory and childish mimicry, perceived by Charlotte and the captain as "strange" and "unexpected," arouses their own desire ("this strange unexpected event . . . [like] the behaviour of children which, because of its consequences, you cannot exactly approve of" [80]). Ottilie goes so far as to write like Eduard, in an amorous mimeography of desire that will take him by surprise.

In the scene of physical abandon between Eduard and Charlotte, the characters are under the intoxicating influence of mimetic confusion. The imagined shadows of their rivals add a hallucinatory dimension to the scene. The absence of these other partners is in fact the key to the delirious, vertiginous quality this ultimate union acquires: "In the lamplit twilight inner inclination at once asserted its rights, imagination at once asserted its rights over reality. Eduard held Ottilie in his arms. The Captain hovered back and forth before the soul of Charlotte. The absent and the present were in a miraculous way entwined, seductively and blissfully, each with the other" (106).

Although division prevails at the beginning, the (unconscious) goal of the players is to establish a more harmonious arrangement. The disorder and instability initially created by the captain's arrival eventually result in a new order, a more desirable alliance. This is how Eduard explains the interest afforded by the "complexity" of affinities: "the affinities become interesting only when they bring about divorces" (53). The contractual (cultural) harmony of marriage is somehow transcended by a more "natural" affinity between spirits: this is the "higher determination" (55), as the captain explains, that is couched in the chemical metaphor. The adulterous quartet is bound by fate, as if the new harmony had been foretold, predestined. It is in this sense that Goethe's text is the reverse of Laclos's libertine monadology, in which the goal was to arrive at increasingly divided formations, at an overriding disharmony of the whole through fatal seductions.

Goethe's text seems thus far to avoid the crisis provoked in *Les Liaisons*. At times, it is true, the mimetic desire of the characters comprises an element of hate, as in the captain's hypocritical antipathy toward Eduard's music. The moments when the four characters are together, in silent mimetic confrontation, can become unbearable. Still, although Goethe does set up the danger of the sacrificial crisis, he dismantles it when its conditions have been met. The captain's zeal, his hyperactivity, the new economy he imposes on the household are meant to spare the collectivity, to rebuild it. Although his pursuits can be seen as typical eighteenth-century activities (gardening, cataloging, classifying), we must consider the essentially anthropological function of his work. The captain's wish to saturate time and fill up space in these ways betrays his fear of discord, his eagerness to reforge bonds.

Even festivities take on the bonding function in Goethe's novel. The danger of their going amiss is obvious: "A calm evening, not a breath of wind, all seemed right for the nocturnal festival, when suddenly a terrible shrieking and shouting started up. Big lumps of earth had come away from the dam, several people could be seen falling into the water" (125). The ground the collective stands on is fragile, "uneven and insecure" (124), like the dams where the people crowd together: "The earth had given way under the pressure and trampling of the ever-increasing crowd. Everyone wanted the best position and now no one could go forward or back" (125). The crowd's blind confusion after the peaceful festivities, the arousal of rivalries, and the trampled soil all mime a silent violence, the contagion of the mob. But Goethe soon restores order. Everyone will be saved, thanks precisely to collective action. The crowd's return to harmony even makes a sacrifice unnecessary. A little boy who was carried off far from the dam and nearly drowned is saved during this sort of collective baptism. "Everyone has been saved" (126), the captain is reassured.

The construction scene fully exposes the ritual birthing of the community. The architectural and masonic metaphor preaches the unity of the collective: "for, as men who are naturally inclined to one another hold together better when they are cemented by the law, so too bricks whose shapes are already well matched are better united by this binding force" (83). The successful collective should efface these forces through its harmonious functioning: the links should be internalized, invisible. The collective must give the effect of an organic, seamless whole, a palimpsest with all traces of heterogeneity smoothed over: "The square-cut foundation is choked with earth, and even the walls we build in the light of day in the end almost disappear from mind. The work of the stonecutter and the sculptor are most visible to view, and we are even compelled to approve when the decorator obliterates the traces of our labour altogether and appropriates our work to himself by overlaying, smoothing and painting it" (84).

Elective Affinities differs from the previous texts we have studied because it rejects the seduction of ornamentation. We are witness, even, to the sacrificial expulsion of adornment from the collective. The same construction scene contains this second *foundational* ritual. The women decide to bury their accoutrements of coquetry: everything that bears the mark of the individual, of narcissistic ostentation, is interred for the good of the collective:

> The ladies offered their hair-combs, and smelling-bottles and other trinkets went in. Ottilie alone, sunk in contemplation of the offerings, failed to give anything, until a word from Eduard brought her back and then she unfastened from around her neck the gold chain from which her father's picture had hung and laid it gently on top of the other treasures, and after she had done that Eduard hastily had the covering slab put on and fixed at once. (85)

We would have to go back to *La Nouvelle Héloïse* to find such a forceful magnetic atmosphere, such a contagious air of seduction. In Rousseau's novel, Julie is the one whose charms have such a strong effect on the community. She is like a magician of transparency and harmony. Rousseau has her exhaust herself in various rituals, festivities, and ceremonies that serve to found the community and pull it together. Rousseau himself writes that

> I have observed that in a very intimate group the styles and characters of the members become so close that as their souls become confounded, so do their ways of thinking, feeling and saying. This Julie, such as she is, must be an enchanting creature: everybody that comes near her must resemble her; everything around her must become Julie; all her friends must adopt but one tone.[4]

Jean Starobinski, following Burgelin's lead, has convincingly analyzed this passage, identifying Julie's behavior as an *influence*, a contagion communicated from consciousness to consciousness. This sympathetic power Julie exhibits can be explained by mimesis. Starobinski cites another illuminating passage from Rousseau: "Spirits of a certain temper . . . transform others into themselves, so to speak; they possess a sphere of activity within which nothing can resist them: to know them is to want to imitate them."[5] Julie provides the model for Clarens; she is a mediator, in the strongest sense of the term. She stands mysteriously at the center of everyone's desires: as a lover (to Saint-Preux), as a daughter (to Monsieur d'Etange), as a wife (to Monsieur de Wolmar). Paternal incest in fact condenses the magnetic orientation of desires toward Julie. The father's desire for his daughter and the violent jealousy that ensues might even be said to copy Saint-Preux's desire for Julie. Saint-Preux's arrival in the d'Etange household fixes Julie as the object of desire. Indeed, the person who appears before the astonished eyes of the father is his idealized daughter, transformed by the seductive private tutor: "my father admired no less my progress in music and drawing . . . he was very happy with all my talents."[6] The father is later condemned to repeat this incestuous posture when he finds his daughter a husband who resembles him (a twenty-year friendship has made them inseparable companions; Rousseau's text tells us that Monsieur d'Etange "hoped to make a son-in-law of his friend" [252]).

This mimetic schema sketched by Rousseau is a reversal of the patriarchal economy that forces the father to find a spouse for his daughter and denies her any possibility of choice. Rousseau shows here that the father's incestuous tendency has a mimetic motivation. It is not the daughter who is attached to her father, as the oedipal schema would have it, but, rather, the father who is attached to his daughter. The daughter submits to her father's desire only after the fact. Rousseau shows that families create an intense mimetic theater, made fragile by a potential for all sorts of upheavals. To fixate on one particular abnormal constellation, as psychoanalysis does, is to indulge in an arbitrary exercise.

The ending of Rousseau's novel transforms the characters into doubles. Saint-Preux latches on to the new husband in an extremely odd fashion, forming a strange *ménage à trois*. He confides: "their influence wins me over and moves me insensibly, and my heart gradually joins with theirs, just as one's voice, unbeknownst to oneself, takes on the tone of those with whom one speaks" (398). The same observation is repeated further on: "I understood from the way her husband squeezed my hand, that the same emotion had taken sway over all three of us, and that the sweet influence of that expansive soul [Julie] took effect all around her" (423).

Similarly, there is a sort of cloning of Julie: her cousin Claire takes the heroine's place next to her lover—or at least this is Julie's deathbed wish ("what delight for me to unite two hearts so well made for each other, and which have melded for so long with mine!" (480). Henriette, Claire's daughter, takes over from the deceased. The girl, who has an uncanny way of imitating Julie's gestures and voice, is purposely adorned to complete the resemblance.

Although Julie's mediation is successful in founding a magnetic community, she pays for it heavily, through an enormous sacrifice: She becomes the scapegoat of the group (sublimating her love for Saint-Preux, Julie gives herself over to the conjugal economy and the most virtuous maternity). Starobinski correctly perceived it as a fleshly sacrifice of her own body in the violent death that strikes her at the end of the novel. Julie becomes sullied, contaminated, and the community must quickly protect itself. The magic power that she exercised over her little group gives her death ceremony a profoundly bizarre atmosphere, provokes the hallucination of her return from the afterworld, and surrounds her death with superstitious fears. Rousseau laces these scenes with a heavy dose of archaism, which would explain the supernatural dimension of his heroine's seductive capacity.

This sort of generalized mimesis leaves its oddest traces in Goethe's text, where it is incarnated in Charlotte's child, Otto. He monstrously resembles all four of the partners: he bears the name of the father and the friend; he has Ottilie's eyes. Otto was, as the text says, "begotten in twofold adultery" (260). In fact, he is an exact copy of the perverse phantasy that conceived him. Let us recall the famous scene in which Eduard and Charlotte make love: "In the lamplit twilight inner inclination at once asserted its rights, imagination at once asserted its rights over reality. Eduard held Ottilie in his arms. The Captain hovered back and forth before the soul of Charlotte. The absent and the present were in a miraculous way entwined, seductively and blissfully, each with the other" (106). In order to arrest this contagious mimesis and restore the principle of differentiation, in order to expiate the evil that has gripped the community, Ottilie and Otto must in the end die.

Ottilie's Eyes

Seduction is a deadly, insidious *actio in distans*. Ottilie's face is in some sense the mute, mysterious face of maleficent seduction. She makes her presence invisible by bewitching Eduard. The mysterious charm of her distance is what colors the end of the novel and marks it with a series of catastrophes (the death of Charlotte's and Eduard's child, Eduard's suicide, and Ottilie's own death). It is as if behind Ottilie lurked Luciane, Charlotte's diabolical daughter, her luminous twin.

Ottilie is present in the novel as a contaminant. She transforms all the relations in her midst by the mystery of her gaze. And it is Ottilie who innocently—out of a desire to possess him—kills Otto, the child of Eduard and Charlotte, her adoptive mother. Walter Benjamin's marvelously insightful reading of the *Affinities* points out the ambiguity of Ottilie. Benjamin writes: "Goethe has endowed Ottilie with the dangerous magic that is peculiar to innocence, and this magic is perfectly suited to her role as sacrificial victim."[7] The images with which Benjamin adorns her, which make up the magical apparition that she is, nevertheless require reinforcement. Ottilie's innocence harbors within it the mystery of her evil: she is secretly nocturnal. Better than anyone else, Benjamin conveys the paradoxical nature that is at the heart of her seduction: "A soul whose innocent limpidity seduces and plunges others into the darkest shadows" (100). Benjamin gives all this archaism a lyrical, romantic interpretation, which I believe needs to be taken literally. Benjamin speaks repeatedly of "demoniacal principles of incantatory magic [that] irrupt into the work" (96), of "the bewitchment of form" (98). But it is to Desire that this magical dimension must be restored. The mystery that accompanies Ottilie, and which makes her a goddess of appearances, a living icon, a high priestess of the image must be seen not only as an aesthetic culmination but also as the fatal knowledge of desire. She who holds herself apart as the inaccessible object of desire, however, sees the torment resulting from the noncoincidence of desire and the subject of desire (from not being at the locus of her desire). This is what she expresses through the metaphor of the architect's profession. The architect is as if dispossessed, alienated from his own work. Pacing alongside the work, unable to contemplate *jouissance* in it, he is like the father of a child lost forever. When Ottilie sees the places where Eduard, now absent, would have wished to be, her suffering is dominated by this nonpossession, this impossibility of *jouissance*.

The mimetic quartet is organized around Ottilie: she is at its center, as the image of desire. She is also the most unhappy victim of its cruelty. As soon as she arrives, the gatherings become more and more frequent; topics of conversation are chosen specially with her participation in mind; her presence is silently awaited at the table. Goethe's text clearly states the degree to which Ottilie is the instigator of improved communication and stability in the group. In the inconsistency of Ottilie's innocence Benjamin sees something on the order of the false pretense, of the façade.[8] It could be said that the mystery of Ottilie's coquetry lies in the distance she maintains, in the confusion with which she offers herself up to the other's gaze, in the ambiguity of the gift she makes of herself. She enthralls the architect, who creates images of her, surrounding her with a sacred aura, transforming her into an unreal divinity, a "queen of the heavens." Ottilie herself acts out a pantomime of holiness verging so closely on the truth that the scene leaves its witnesses with a strange and disturbing feeling of anxiety. In a humorous vein, even the magnetic pendulum demonstrated by one of Charlotte's visitors reacts wildly to Ottilie's presence.

The perfect mediator of desire, Ottilie is adept at making herself simultaneously available and aloof in her secret. Her coquetry is held at a distance from herself like the adornments that Eduard gives her, which she prefers to keep as objects of contemplation: she will wear them only on the day of her death. Like our seductresses, she has curative powers (Benjamin points out that by invoking the saint of the same name, she restores sight),[9] but this power to cure also brings on misfortune. If Ottilie causes illness, she is herself the first to suffer from the malady that she carries—passion, this disease that, she says in her journal, is incurable and that all remedies merely serve to aggravate: a strange pharmacy, fraught with danger! It is in her eyes that Ottilie seems to carry this incurable affliction—those eyes that mesmerize the architect and Eduard and that are fatefully transmitted to Otto, the child of adulterous desire.[10] No sooner has she seen him and, terrified, discovered the incandescence of her own image in his eyes, than he is doomed to die.

From the distance of her gaze, Ottilie transfixes.

A Little Goddess

Part Two of *Elective Affinities* brings us back to a more "French" novelistic vein, with the return of coquetry and the reign of adornment and representation. It is dominated by Luciane, who transforms it into an exact inverse of the first. Within the frame of the novel itself, Ottilie and Charlotte contemplate this complete metamorphosis along with us, the readers. The characters' busy employment of the first part, their ritual work, is supplanted by leisure. Leisure is pure mobility, with no purpose or destination (trips, dances, gaming, balls, festivities): "Luciane still continued to appear like a flaming comet drawing a long tail behind it" (174). She reigns over her world like a super-coquette: "she had provided herself with endless changes of clothes" (175); "the maidservants . . . were never finished with washing and ironing, mending and stitching" (174).

If Part One of *Elective Affinities* was a foundational narrative (the ritual festivities partook of the collective's esprit de corps), in Part Two gallantry, wordly ostentation, and the social whirlwind once again prevail. Space is invaded by Society ("Her court expanded with every day that passed" [183]), saturated by the din and tumult of the Court. Centered around the captain in the first part of the novel, society seemed to find a meaning, whereas here Luciane uses her Medusa-like powers to transfix the company. She makes a spectacle of herself in bizarre stagings. The sacred ceremonies of the first part are replaced by the profane festivities that she institutes in the second. The coquette, now an astute politician, makes herself into an object of idolatry. Luciane's mother Charlotte had already warned us about the girl's "innately commanding personality" and the charm exerted over others by this "little goddess" (29).

The text now becomes preoccupied with *image*. These discussions focus on the representation of the persona as phantasm and idol. Idolatrous representation and cult worship supplant the naturalistic representation (classification, grouping, arrangement of nature and the collective) that characterized the beginning. The community, now under the diabolical sway of representation, is gripped by the vision of the persona. Luciane appears bizarrely costumed in various tableaux: as Artemisia, queen of Caria, "she reappeared to the sad caressing tones of the death-march" (176). Luciane the actress appears in two other tableaux. Goethe's text describes the hypnotic fascination she exercises on the crowd in *Esther before Ahasuerus*: "In the figure of the unconscious swooning queen she was able to display all her attractions, and she had prudently selected for the maidens surrounding and supporting her only girls who, while pretty and shapely enough, could not for a moment endure comparison with her" (191). A similar effect is achieved in *Instruction paternelle*: "This picture was to be the occasion for Luciane to exhibit herself at her very best. Her braids and the shape of her head and neck were lovely beyond conception, and her figure . . . was wonderfully slim and dainty and light, and was shown to the greatest advantage in the older costume" (192).

Luciane, endowed with all the talents of a master hypnotist, is a veritable Mesmer. Her theatrical appearances are crafted using all the magnetic techniques of the period. Not only a coquette, she is also a sorceress, performing her witchery under the guise of her sensational theatrics. Luciane also wields her mimetic talent over others. Goethe's text presents her as a strange sort of pharmacist:

> She seemed to have made it a rule to be, not only cheerful with the cheerful, but also sad with the sad and, faithful to the spirit of contradiction, sometimes to annoy the cheerful and cheer the sad. Whenever she visited a family she asked about the sick and infirm who were unable to join the company. She visited them in their room, played the doctor and pressed upon them the powerful physic she kept in the travelling medicine-chest which accompanied her everywhere; whether such a cure failed or succeeded was, as might be imagined, a matter of chance. (192–93)

But there is one event above all that ends up giving her a bad reputation. This scene has all the appearances of a seance or a magnetic ritual, but it later takes on a distinctly sacrificial dimension. Luciane manages to provoke a recurrence of hysteria and persecution mania in one of her patients. As if unbeknownst to her, the cure (*pharmakos*) turns into a poison:

> One of the daughters of a respected house had had the misfortune to be responsible for the death of one of her younger brothers and was unable to get over it. . . . Luciane had heard of this and she at once secretly resolved that when she came to visit that house she would, as it were, perform a miracle and restore the girl to society. She bore herself more circumspectly than usual, managed to gain access to the mentally sick patient and, as far as anyone could tell, win her confidence by talking about and playing music. But finally she made a mistake, for,

> because she wanted as always to produce a sensation, she one evening brought the pale beautiful child, whom she thought she had sufficiently prepared, unexpectedly out into a noisy glittering assemblage; and perhaps this too would have been a success had the company itself not behaved ineptly out of curiosity and apprehension, crowding around the invalid and then avoiding her and making her confused and agitated by whispering and putting their heads together. The highly-strung girl could not endure it. She fled, emitting fearful shrieks that sounded like cries of terror at some approaching demon. The company scattered in alarm. (198–99)

The collective, thus gathered in readiness to victimize the young girl in silence, appears in all its monstrousness; but it reacts as if the girl's terror came from some other source. The fact is, Luciane's plan backfires. We now understand why Goethe has Luciane appear in all her various disguises, like a fairy-tale character. A talented mime, she is above all a sorceress, privy to the secrets of the soul. As peasant or flower-girl, fairy or mermaid, "she so confounded the actual with the imaginary that you really thought you were dealing with the Saalnixe [nymph of the hall]" (175).

Luciane: Lucifer.

Exit

Goethe, *Faust*

Faust's restless yearning is a desire for divinity. At the beginning of Goethe's poem, surrounded by his little world steeped in knowledge ("Hemmed in with stacks of books am I, / Where works the worm with dusty mange / While to the vaulted roof on high / The smoky ranks of papers range"[1]), Faust sinks into a sort of cosmic hallucination. Drunk with divinity, he wishes as God's image to be His equal: "Myself a god?" (45). In the midst of his infernal laboratory, Faust mimics God's creation: the room vaults upward like the heavens. Goethe makes the hero of his poem a hybrid creature, mixing magician (alchemist) and Freemason. Faust is the hyperdiabolical ancestor of Goethe's captain-chemist and of the sorceress-cum-pharmacist Luciane.

As a god, Faust commands worship. He wreaks on the mob the diabolical seduction of the scientific witch-doctor. The cure, the mimetic opposite of poisoning, expresses an intense craving for the other. The subject who desires the cure is diseased—infected with the other. Illness is the passive, submissive form that desire takes before the model. Faust is addressed by the peasants: "And you, a young man in those days, / Took every plague-house in your round" (64). His companion, Wagner, describes as follows the mob's attention:

> What feelings, Sir, your heart must realize,
> To see the tribute of the wondering crowd!

> Happy the man commanding such a prize
> By gifts with which his genius is endowed!
> The father shows to you his little son,
> And where you walk the people stand and stare,
> The eager wonder seizes everyone,
> The fiddler pauses and the dance is done,
> And people cheer, and hats fly in the air.
> A little more, and down they'd kneel, almost
> As if the priest had raised the sacred Host. (64)

Faust himself admits to his Satanic seduction, his diabolical descent:

> And now this praise means mockery and blame.
> If only you could read within my soul,
> How little sire or son can truly claim
> The virtues that these simple folk extol!
> My father worked with honour none too clear,
> Poring on Nature and her dark dominion,
> An ardent scholar, with a mind sincere,
> Yet crossed with cranks and obstinate opinion.
> In company of choice practitioners
> He tended cauldrons of the midnight crew.
> From countless secret recipes these sirs
> Concocted fearful things of foulest brew. . . .
> So, with a nostrum of this hellish sort,
> We made these hills and valleys our resort,
> And ravaged there more deadly than the pest.
> These hands have ministered the deadly bane
> To thousands who have perished; I remain
> To hear cool murderers extolled and bless'd. (65)

Mephistopheles' temptation, his satanic seduction, occupies the locus of this desire for divinity by flattering this desire. In *Faust*, the devil is the *parasite*. First he comes to inhabit Faust's home, as his double: Mephistopheles dons Faust's clothing as a camouflage the better to dictate his desires—all the while passing himself off as Faust's servant. The devil may be selfish, as Faust says, but he is hypocritical, for he feigns altruism, mimicking the other's interests. Madame de Staël perceived this particularity of Faust's seduction with marvelous clarity: "What he means by seduction is catering to the other's passions."[2] She saw seduction as this particular form of mediating relationship.

It is impossible to understand Faust's seduction of Margareta without first clarifying Mephistopheles' mediating relation to Faust—the first seduction. The devil comes to occupy the locus of Faust's double desire. First, there is Faust's intellectualized desire. As Nerval so clearly saw, there is a movement from human desires to absolute desire, the desire for science and for possession through imagination—a desire to be God. But the devil arouses not only this desire for transcendence; through his mediation, Faust also discovers the terrestrial form of seduction, the demoniacal torture of passion ("Blundering with desire towards fruition, / And in fruition pining for desire" [146]). It is through Mephistopheles' intervention that Faust comes to desire and to obtain Margareta. Made young again by means of a philter, Faust sees the idealized image of woman appear in the sorceress's mirror. Later, Mephistopheles will succeed in seducing Margareta for his master. The casket of jewels he secretly leaves in her wardrobe has the desired effect on the young woman: she is indeed seduced by these objects; the devil has awakened in her the charms of coquetry, an indulgence encouraged, and shared, by her neighbor Martha: "Come often over here to me, / And dress up fine where none can see, / And walk before the mirror here, A joy for both of us, my dear" (131). Thus does Mephistopheles prepare his master's seduction of Margareta. Faust need only follow in his footsteps and imitate his gestures.

Mephistopheles' role as go-between is revealed above all in the way he later on insinuates himself between the two lovers as an obstacle, a rival of the desire he himself has helped create between the two characters. He seeks to regain this enviable place of desire. This replay of the original seduction does not escape Faust: "You snake of snakes!" (148). Like a voyeur, the devil insinuates himself between the two lovers who are bewitched by passion, reciprocally possessed: "I've envied you indeed / Those twin delights that in the roses feed" (149).

The power of Goethe's poem resides above all in the way it is able to carry seductive mediation to the point of paroxysm, giving it the hyperbolic form of the devil-double, both instigator of and obstacle to desire, who ends up desiring for himself the object he had placed before Faust's wonderstruck eyes. Thus does the poem speak the truth of desire. Mephisto, as initiator, sniffs out Faust's self-annihilation and in this night sets up shop. Indeed, it is in this nothingness that desire will find its most powerful motivations and its most illusory pretentions: they are the shadow cast by desire. In its extreme form as desire for glory and transcendence, in its vanity, desire is the deceitful, hypocritical echo of this original lack. To forget his fragility, the subject of desire wishes to incorporate all the desires of others. What results is the erotomania of the coquette or the naive vanity of Marivaux's Jacob—but also the paroxysmal figure of the political seducer of later texts: Crébillon, Laclos, Sade, and Goethe. Marivaux's intoxicating vanity becomes the vertigo of divinity; seductive flirting is transformed into a desire for domination.

The addictive power of the multiple, which is also the seducer's distinguishing trait (he wants all women, desires all desires), in fact hides his annulment, his failure to belong to himself. If the seducer offers the world an enhanced desire, this delegation leads ultimately to the sacrifice of his person. This vicariousness *voids* him. . . . The separation indicated by the etymology of the word *seduction* thus affects not only those beings who are touched by seduction's evil eye but also the seducer himself. By holding himself up as model to the other, by feigning not to have a model of his own or to be his own model, the seducer comes face to face in the falseness of this mimetic reflexivity with his own void, the echo of his suffering ego, the vacuity of his showy façade. The separation the Sadean seducer experiences at the center of his pleasure is even more radical, because it is conscious. The hateful schism of the self in Sade reveals the impossibility of fulfilling others' desires; for the glimmer of divinity glimpsed in the other's face constitutes an insurmountable obstacle.

It is not difficult to understand how Goethe, at the twilight of the Enlightenment, was able to conceive his Faust. He gave his seducer the face of Satan, the duplicity of the devil; he supplemented the seducer's desires with the appropriate measure of evil. The poem ends with a chorus of bacchantes, a witches' sabbath celebrated to the accompaniment of the devil's roar. The entire century is summed up in Faust's diabolical alchemy, in the twilight song of these nocturnal beings, in the hell that descends and ravishes the devout Margareta.

Goethe's drama has been intellectualized, with Faust's desire for divinity seen as the arrogance and the agony of genius; his passion for Margareta has been psychologized as a form of self-torture. But these approaches deliberately deprive Faust of his desire. I propose to restore to the text all the archaism that modernity has stifled. Madame de Staël, with an almost Baudelairian intuition in her readiness to breathe in *Faust*'s Satanic emanations, was receptive to the play's archaism: she saw in it "a powerful witchery, a wickedness of principle, an intoxication with evil, a deviance of thought, that chill the heart."[3] Certainly, the desire for seduction is highly intellectualized in Faust, but Margareta's reflection, her entrapment in the mirror, fully conveys the power of temptation, the torment of absence.

In Faust's words we must read the scandal of desire, its infinite march toward the light, however inseparable it is from the darkness: "Dawn softens night, the deepest shades are fled" (193).

NOTES

The Mirrored Bedroom

1. Jean Baudrillard, *Seduction*, trans. Brian Singer (New York: St. Martin's Press, 1990), 1.

2. *Reflections on the Novel*, in *The 120 Days of Sodom and Other Writings*, trans. Austryn Winhouse and Richard Seaver (New York: Grove Press, 1966), 99.

3. Monique Schneider makes a similar observation; see her "La Séduction comme parure ou comme initiation," *Traverses* 17 (1979), 31–44.

4. Jean-Didier Vincent, *Casanova. La Contagion du plaisir* (Paris: Odile Jacob, 1990), 150. On these occult aspects of the eighteenth century, see pp. 148–64.

5. See Humbert de Gallier, *Filles nobles et magiciennes* (Paris: Calmann-Lévy, 1913). On Casanova, see the superb book by Chantal Thomas, *Casanova. Un voyage libertin* (Paris: Denöel, 1985).

6. "In their report to the King in 1784, physicians attributed the effect of magnetism to the imagination of the sick, to the spirit of imitation that makes public performances so dangerous, since the sight of one person having a fit could provoke a convulsion in another." In Ernest d'Hauterive, *Le Merveilleux au XVIIIe siècle* (Paris: Juven, 1902), 209. See also Robert Darnton, *Mesmerism and the End of the Enlightenment in France* (Cambridge, Mass.: Harvard University Press, 1968). The verb *to mesmerize* has preserved the meaning of fascination.

7. Gérard de Nerval, *Œuvres*, II (Paris: Gallimard, Pléiade, 1966), 1135.

8. "Un Si Cruel Savoir," *Critique* 18(182) (1962): 606–607. In *Histoire de la folie à l'âge classique*, Foucault denounces the repression (the confinement) of this population. The Age of Enlightenment takes hold as the era of a massive process of standardization and localiza-

tion of *unreason*: "Within the walls of confinement could be found a mixture of syphilitics, debauchees, would-be sorceresses, alchemists, libertines. . . . From guilt and sexual pathos, to ancient rites of invocation and magic, to sleight-of-hand and to the delirious laws of the heart, an underground network takes shape, sketching the contours of the secret foundations of madness." Michel Foucault, *Histoire de la folie à l'âge classique* (Paris: Gallimard, Tel, 1972), 119.

9. "By my gaze, I touch, I reach, I seize, I am seized." Roland Barthes, *L'Obvie et l'obtus* (Paris: Seuil, 1982), 279.

10. See Søren Kierkegaard, "The Immediate Erotic Stages," in *Either/Or*, I, trans. Howard V. Hong and Edna H. Hong (Princeton, N.J.: Princeton University Press, 1987), 107–108.

11. "Rape, Seduction, Psychoanalysis," in *Rape*, ed. Sylvana Tomaselli and Roy Porter (New York: Basil Blackwell, 1986), 82.

12. *Things Hidden since the Foundation of the World*, trans. Stephen Bann and Michael Metteer (Stanford, Ca.: Stanford University Press, 1987), 304.

13. Paisley Livingston, *Models of Desire: René Girard and the Psychology of Mimesis* (Baltimore: Johns Hopkins University Press, 1992), 1.

14. Ibid., 39 and 42.

15. René Girard, *Deceit, Desire, and the Novel*, trans. Yvonne Freccero (Baltimore: Johns Hopkins University Press, 1965), 56.

16. *L'Amour inconscient* (Paris: Grasset, 1983), 68.

17. "La Séduction en psychanalyse," *Etudes Freudiennes* 27 (1986): 144.

18. Cf. René Girard, *Things Hidden*, especially Part 3, chap. 2, "Desire without Object."

19. H. Hubert and Marcel Mauss, *Mélange d'histoire des religions* (Paris: Alcan, 1909), 185.

20. Quoted by Chantal Thomas, *Casanova*, 277.

21. Roland Barthes, *Sade, Fourier, Loyola*, trans. Richard Miller (New York: Farrar, Straus, & Giroux, 1976), 146.

22. Baudrillard, *Seduction*, 69.

23. Ibid., 101.

24. Ibid. (emphasis added).

25. On the subject of magnetism, see Jean-Michel Oughourlian's *Un Mime nommé désir* (Paris: Grasset, 1982).

Of Coquetry

1. All quotations are from Pierre Carlet de Chamberlain de Marivaux, *The Virtuous Orphan or, the Life of Marianne Countess of *****: An Eighteenth-Century English Translation by Mrs. Mary Mitchell Collyer of Marivaux's La Vie de Marianne*, edited with a critical introduction by William Harlin McBurney and Michael Francis Shugrue. Copyright © 1965 by Southern Illinois University Press. Passages cited from the French edition (indicated by "M") are translated directly from *La Vie de Marianne* (Paris: Garnier, 1963).

2. *Coquetry* is an interesting word. It comes from *coquet* (little rooster or cock). Although it designates an activity recognized as essentially feminine, originally it indicated male display. Woman thus borrowed the phallic seduction of the opposite sex (through rivalry), and right from the beginning man felt the need to exhibit that which he lacked.

3. Jacques Lacan, *Ecrits*, II (Paris: Seuil, 1971), 113. On the question of the masquerade, see also Judith Butler, *Gender Trouble* (New York: Routledge, 1990), 43–57.

4. Marivaux, *Le Cabinet du philosophe*, in *Journaux et œuvres diverses* (Paris: Garnier, 1969), 377–78.

5. Luce Irigaray, *Sexes et parentés* (Paris: Editions de Minuit, 1987), 77.

6. Friedrich Nietzsche, *The Gay Science*, trans. Walter Kaufmann (New York: Vintage, 1974), par. 71, pp. 127–28.

7. Freud, *New Introductory Lectures on Psychoanalysis*, trans. James Strachey (New York: Norton, 1965), 132. Between Freud and Nietzsche, Stendhal writes that women "commit themselves" through finery, thus rectifying their natural chasteness. Cf. *De l'amour* (Paris: Gallimard, Folio, 1980), 83.

8. Dolls can be viewed as a narcissistic projection of the little girl, as an identificatory mimicking of the imaginary model of womanhood. Rousseau sees playing with dolls as the origin of coquetry, a precocious and almost natural "hunger for adornments": "Watch a little girl spending time with her doll, constantly adjusting her fit, clothing her, unclothing her a hundred times or more, continually seeking new combinations of ornaments . . . but, you will say, she is adorning her doll, and not herself; quite true; she sees her doll, and does not see herself . . . she is entirely caught up in her doll, she applies all her coquetry to it . . . she awaits the moment in which she herself will

become the doll." Quoted by Alain Grosrichard, "Le Prince saisi par la philosophie," *Ornicar?* 26–27 (1983): 144.

9. On Marianne's Pascalian leanings, see Leo Spitzer's comment in "A propos de *La Vie de Marianne*," in *Etudes de style* (Paris: Gallimard, 1970), 381.

10. *Translator's note*: A lapsus is literally a "falling down"; a *faux pas* is a "false step."

11. Marianne had already been designated as a sexual object by the monk who recommended her to Climal. In fact, the monk anticipates the seduction of Marianne's future "benefactor": "And to excite him more effectually, he mentioned my sex, my age and beauty, with the fatal consequences they might possibly have, either from my own weakness or the wickedness of others" (24).

12. See Jean Baudrillard, *L'Echange symbolique et la mort* (Paris: Gallimard, 1976), especially chap. 4, "Le Corps ou le charnier de signes."

13. On the castrating gaze of the woman I refer to Freud's essay "Medusa's Head," in *The Complete Psychological Works of Sigmund Freud*, trans. James Strachey, vol. 18 (London: Hogarth Press, 1955), 273–74. I follow here the interpretations that locate the terror of the Medusa in the return of the woman's look; on the way she defies the gaze of the male other, cf. the article by Beth Newman, "'The Situation of the Looker-On': Gender, Narration, and Gaze in *Wuthering Heights*," *PMLA* 105(5) (1990): 1030–31.

14. The cap, which appears several times in the text, comes in some sense to symbolize all feminine adornments. It is the sign of beautification and femininity. Marianne takes it off during the scene in which she shows Climal her disheveled hair. Hiding the head of hair, the cap would appear to conceal a primitive, natural femininity. It is the sign of culture, re-erected—perhaps a displaced protection against the forbidden display of pubic hair?

15. Marivaux uses this phrase in *Le Spectateur français*, in *Journaux*, 125.

16. *Le spectateur français* in *Journaux*, 118. Michel Deguy complicates the seductive mechanism of this scene. For him, the lack of intimacy is characterized by a narcissistic theft: the spectator "is jealous because he could not take the place of the mirror, this obscure hunger of the young woman that makes her ceaselessly seek out the reflection of her image—and nothing else . . . the spectator would have liked to 'narcissize' her, to take the place of this thing that she prefers over all others: the shining surface for her reflection." In *La Machine matrimoniale de Marivaux* (Paris: Gallimard, 1986), 27.

17. See the excellent article on this subject by Piera Aulagnier-Spairani, "Remarques sur la féminité et ses avatars," in *Le Désir et la perversion* (Paris: Seuil, 1967): 53–79.

18. *Le Cabinet du philosophe*, 371.

19. Ibid., 374–75.

20. Ibid., 373.

21. "La Féminité," 76.

22. Sarah Kofman, *The Enigma of Woman*, trans. Catherine Porter (Ithaca, N.Y.: Cornell University Press, 1985). See especially "Narcissistic Woman," 50–65.

23. René Girard, *Things Hidden since the Foundation of the World*, trans. Stephen Bann and Michael Metteer (Stanford, Ca.: Stanford University Press, 1987), 370 (emphasis added).

24. Mikkel Borch-Jacobsen, *The Freudian Subject* (Stanford, Ca.: Stanford University Press, 1988), 111–112.

25. *Le Cabinet*, 374. Milan Kundera sexualizes the distancing effect of coquetry: "What is flirtation? One might say that it is behavior leading another to believe that sexual intimacy is possible, while preventing that possibility from becoming a certainty. In other words, flirting is a promise of sexual intercourse without a guarantee." In *The Unbearable Lightness of Being*, trans. Michael Henry Heim (New York: Harper & Row, 1984), 142. For Georg Simmel, this hesitation, this *perhaps*, is undoubtedly coquetry's greatest power. But Simmel tends to essentialize womanhood in the game of the promise, in this art that makes her oscillate between a yes and a no, this privilege of alternative. See his *Philosophie de la modernité* (Paris: Payot, 1989), 205–29.

26. See Michael Fried's *Absorption and Theatricality* (Berkeley: University of California Press, 1980) on the dramatic spectacle of absorption in eighteenth-century painting.

27. This adoption through seduction must be understood in the context of the first separation that constitutes Marianne's very being: the loss of her parents. The scene that marks the absence of Marianne's birth is paradoxically given by Marivaux as a delivery, a birth. The mother's blood covers the drowning body of the child:

> A stagecoach on the road to Bordeaux was attacked by villains. . . . Two of the gentlemen leapt out of the coach and made resistance, but being overpowered by numbers were soon murderd, after having wounded some of the assassins. Two women in the coach, with the postilion and coachman, shared the same

> unhappy fate, and there only remained alive a canon of Sens and I . . . who seemed to be between two or three years old. The canon fled, while I, who had fallen down in the coach, was screaming and crying in the most dreadful manner, being half smothered under the body of one of the women, who, wounded and unable to support herself, fell upon me and in her expiring agonies almost crushed me to death. . . . [T]he lady lay with one side of her face upon mine, which she had bathed with blood. . . . They removed the lady, forced me from her arm, and took me out of the coach almost drowned in blood. (pp. 8–9)

Stagecoach, crossroads, villains: this episode could easily be read as a female œdipal narrative. What is absolutely certain, in any case, is the role that this story plays for Marianne, who recounts it to everyone she meets. Marianne uses it to construct for herself a "family romance."

Poison

1. Quotations in English are taken from Antoine-François Prévost d'Exiles, *Manon Lescaut*, trans. Leonard Tancock (London: Penguin Classics, 1949), copyright © Leonard Tancock, 1949.

2. Edmond and Jules de Goncourt, *La Femme au XVIIIe siècle* (Paris: Flammarion, 1982), 245.

3. *La Femme au XVIIIe siècle*, 250.

4. See the excellent article by Kristin Ross on Manon as *fascinum*: "The Narrative of Fascination: Pathos and Repetition in *Manon Lescaut*," *The Eighteenth Century* 24(3) (1963): 199–210.

5. Let us remember for our genealogy that Manon is a familiar derivative of Marianne. See *Manon Lescaut*, ed. F. Deloffre and R. Picard (Paris: Garnier, 1965), 21, note 7.

6. Luce Irigaray, *This Sex Which Is Not One*, trans. Catherine Porter (Ithaca: Cornell University Press, 1985), 176.

7. The exemplary reference here on the part of the narrator is a way of suppressing the homosexual overtones of Des Grieux and Tiberge's friendship. On the sexual ambiguity of friendship, see David Halperin's "Heroes and Their Pals," in *One Hundred Years of Homosexuality* (New York: Routledge, 1990).

8. Sigmund Freud, "Contributions to the Psychology of Love,"

trans. Joan Riviere, in *Sexuality and the Psychology of Love*, ed. Philip Rieff (New York: Collier Books, 1963), 51.

9. *Sexuality*, 50.

10. Saint-Preux reproaches Julie in *La Nouvelle Héloïse* for this kind of hypocritical, "inconstant" seduction; she changes her *style* every time she appears: "frolicsome in public . . . serious in private conversation" (Paris: Garnier-Flammarion, 1967), 11.

11. Kristin Ross also stresses this difference between the two lovers. She shows how Prévost's text accentuates the verticality of Des Grieux, to the point of subjecting him to repeated bouts of dizziness, in "Narrative of Fascination," 204.

Forbidden Liaisons

1. Denis Diderot, *The Nun*, trans. Leonard Tancock (London: The Folio Society, 1972).

2. Denis Diderot, *La Religieuse* (Paris: Garnier-Flammarion, 1968), 241. Jean-Claude Bonnet's analysis of Rivette's cinematic adaptation perfectly captures the meaning of the novel: "Suzanne is never able to orient herself. She is constantly denied a space of her own, and this is true starting with the maternal house which, far from being a home, is a hostile and indeterminate place. Later, the convents confront her with discontinuous structures, including a number of obsessive details such as dead-end corridors without any vanishing point, cellars, and the rims around wells. This labile quality of space is only accentuated after Suzanne's liberation. The film transposes the book's ending in a quick-motion cascade, with poor Suzanne tumbling from one place to another, tossed from coach to inn, from farm to laundry, from street to bawdy-house, and reabsorbed in ricochets that ultimately end in the decision to totter in the void." Cf. "Revoir *La Religieuse*," in *Interpréter Diderot aujourd'hui* (Paris: Le Sycomore, 1984), 74–75.

3. We could go back earlier in the narrative. Suzanne's stint as a novitiate is already marked by an initiation into the senses that resonates with the time at Arpajon. The seduction that the novice-mistress directs at Suzanne is similar to the special treatment that the mother superior at Arpajon forces on her. Suzanne refers to this whole operation of "seduction" (26) with a telling term, *fascination* (26), a bewitchment that dominates the other person, submitting him or her to a magical charm. For another reading of the dynamics of seduction in the novel, cf. David Marshall, *The Surprising Effects of*

Sympathy (Chicago: University of Chicago Press, 1988), chap. 3, 84–104.

4. Nietzsche discusses *actio in distans* in "Women and Their Action at a Distance," in *The Gay Science*, trans. Walter Kaufmann (New York: Vintage, 1974), 123–124 (Book 2, section 60).

5. Jacques Lacan, *Les Quatre Concepts fondamentaux de la psychanalyse* (Paris: Seuil, 1973), 107.

6. On the ambiguous relations between Suzanne and the mother superior of Arpajon, see the excellent article by Walter E. Rex, "Secrets from Suzanne: The Tangled Motives of *La Religieuse*," *The Eighteenth Century* 24(3) (1983): 185–98.

7. Walter Benjamin, *Essais*, I, trans. Maurice de Gandillac (Paris: Denoël-Gontheir, 1983), 91.

8. Cf. Michel Foucault, "Sexuality and Solitude," in *On Signs*, ed. M. Blomsky (Baltimore: Johns Hopkins University Press, 1985), 365–72.

9. See Chantal Thomas's wonderful article on this subject: "Les Femmes folles de leurs soeurs," *La Quinzaine littéraire* 418 (1984): 7. But one picture that Suzanne draws for us, of the religious community gathered around its mother superior, contradicts other, horrifying descriptions she gives of the convent as a locus of violent excess due to the concentration of women, a female assembly in the grip of vice. In this exceptional case, what we are shown instead is a gathering of women who are reconciled with one another. The needlework that occupies the nuns is a metaphor for the ties that bind them. Here Diderot brings to life a joyous utopia of female community. The mother superior, the object of adoration, is the one who makes this gathering possible: the community owes its existence to her central position. In contrast to Suzanne's other portrayals, the mother superior appears in this instance to be metamorphosed into a divinity. The specifically feminine character of the nuns' activity (weaving, embroidery, sewing) also reinforces the effect. In the midst of this picture, Suzanne stands out because of her privileged status as a participant and a spectator at the same time ("Everybody was at work except myself" [154]) and as the mother superior's favorite object of attention:

> In the afternoon I went to the Superior's room, where I found quite a large gathering of the youngest and prettiest nuns in the convent; the others had paid their respects and departed. . . .

> Imagine a working party of ten to twelve, the youngest of whom might be fifteen and the oldest not yet twenty-three, a Superior of about forty, white, fresh and plump, sitting up in bed with two chins which she was wearing quite elegantly, arms as round as if they had been turned on a lathe, slender yet dimpled fingers, large black eyes, shining and tender, hardly ever fully open but half closed as though their owner found it rather tiring to open them, lips rosy-red and teeth as white as milk, lovely cheeks and a very handsome head half buried in a deep, soft pillow, her arms spread nonchalantly along her sides, with little cushions supporting each elbow. I was sitting on the edge of her bed doing nothing, but another nun was in an armchair with a little embroidery frame on her knees, while others sat near the windows, making lace. Some were sitting on the floor on cushions taken from the chairs, sewing, embroidering, unpicking embroideries or spinning on a little wheel. . . . The friends were either side by side or opposite each other, and while working they chatted and exchanged advice, looked furtively at each other and linked their fingers on the pretext of giving each other a pin, needle or scissors. The Superior continually ran her eye over them . . . she had the work brought to her and praised or criticized it (153–54).

The scene is later eroticized:

> The Superior rose. She did not sit down with us, but walked round the table, putting her hand on somebody's head and tipping it gently backwards and kissing her on the forehead, pulling up another one's collar and letting her hand linger while pausing to lean against the back of the chair, going on to a third and letting her hand stray over her. . . . Having wandered round a while she stopped opposite me and looked at me with great tenderness and affection. . . . It was a delightful evening (155–56).

10. As an object of desire, Suzanne is irreplaceable. She immediately occupies the center of desires: she is Madame de Moni's favorite, until her position at Longchamp is reversed and she becomes a victim; at Arpajon, she once again immediately becomes the superior's favorite, taking the place previously occupied by Sister Thérèse at the

superior's side. The object of desire is necessarily a separator, and a diabolical one at that. In the embroidery scene, the reason Suzanne paints such a harmonious picture is to secure her own place at the center of attention of both the others and her superior. Sister Thérèse is maliciously excluded, with Suzanne's tacit complicity. Although Suzanne constantly intercedes on her behalf, she does everything to arouse her jealousy: "[The Superior] stopped opposite me and looked at me with great tenderness and affection, but the others kept their eyes lowered as if afraid of inhibiting or distracting her, and especially Sister Sainte-Thérèse" (156). Suzanne takes great pleasure in being this insurmountable object: "The nun who had taken my place gave it back to me" (155).

11. Denis Diderot, *La Religieuse* (Paris: Garnier-Flammarion, 1968), 188.

12. See Sigmund Freud, "A Metaphysical Supplement to the Theory of Dream," in *The Standard Edition*, trans. James Strachey, vol. 14 (London: Hogarth Press, 1957), 223–24.

The Seductive Parasite

1. My reading of the *Peasant* is inspired by Michel Serres's book *Le Parasite* (Paris: Grasset, 1980).

2. Quotations are taken from the translation by Benjamin Boyce (Durham, N.C.: The Seeman Printery, 1974).

3. On the role of clothing with regard to Jacob's progress, cf. Marie-Hélène Huet, *Le Héros et son double* (Paris: Corti, 1975), chap. 2, 31–50.

4. Jacques Lacan, *Les Psychoses* (Paris: Seuil, 1981), 359.

5. Cf. Jean-Joseph Goux, *Symbolic Economies*, trans. Jennifer Curtiss Gage (Ithaca: Cornell University Press, 1989), chap. 1, "Gold and the Phallus," 21–34.

6. But what I am attempting to show here is how the order of desires (the mimetic object) takes precedence over other orders, and how other orders are subordinated to desire and articulated in terms of desire.

The Unquiet Seducer

1. Søren Kierkegaard, "The Immediate Erotic Stages," in *Either/Or*, I, trans. Howard V. Hong and Edna H. Hong (Princeton, NJ: Princeton University Press, 1987), 75–87.

2. Claude Prosper Jolyot de Crébillon, *The Wayward Head and Heart*, trans. Barbara Bray (Oxford: Oxford University Press, 1963). By permission of Oxford University Press.

3. On Casanova's fear, see the fine book by François Roustang, *The Quadrille of Gender*, trans. Anne C. Vila (Stanford, Ca.: Stanford University Press, 1988).

4. Although Hortense may appear as a narcissistic choice of object for Meilcour (she is like the hero's female double, sharing his age and his beauty), she appears less as a spontaneous, original, and romantic choice. She is already caught up in the desire of others. It is as if another desire singles her out. Meilcour is tortured by situations of imaginary jealousy. He sees a potential rival in the young aristocrat Germeuil, but the latter is not alone in the gallery of suitors competing for Meilcour's newfound passion.

5. Seductive dissipation can also be seen as an impossible quest for the irreplaceable mother. See Otto Rank, *Don Juan*, trans. David G. Winter (Princeton, N.J.: Princeton University Press, 1975).

6. Etiemble, in his preface to the French edition, *Les Egarements du cœur et de l'esprit* (Paris: Gallimard, Folio, 1977), 29.

7. On the relation between the ego-ideal and mimesis, see Mikkel Borch-Jacobsen's excellent analysis in *The Freudian Subject* (Stanford, Ca.: Stanford University Press, 1988), 121–23 and 212–15.

8. Shoshana Felman, *The Literary Speech Act: Don Juan with Austin or Seduction in Two Languages* (Ithaca: Cornell University Press, 1983), 31. Claude Reichler writes of the same phenomenon in *La Diabolie* (Paris: Editions de Minuit, 1979). But he studies seduction as a coincidence of phantasies. More precisely, the victim of seduction "always recognizes in it the perfect form of his or her desire—either avowed or secret: he is . . . a prey to his own phantasm, which is beautifully present in front of him in a form that, as he will learn—ever too late and always too soon—is nothing but a decoy" (214).

9. We might say that the fop's mirror is another fop—his imitator, hypocrite, and rival, in relation to whom the fop derives his narcissistic confirmation. This is certainly the role that the Marquis

de Pranzi, Versac's "pupil and constant imitator" (89), plays in *The Wayward Head*.

10. In the same context, one might say that the seducer replaces the *symbolic* order of language (the order of truth) with a *diabolical* order, in which persuasion dominates: in the words of Versac, "the arrangement, or rather the abuse of words, does duty for thought" (167). The seductive word refers only to itself; its rhythm becomes its own mirror, its own deceitful echo. It "makes a great deal of noise" (168); it must speak ill of itself (*mé-dire*, literally "to curse," with a pun on the personal pronoun "*me*"). I am making use here of Claude Reichler's distinction between *sumbolon* (what unites, brings together) and *diabolos* (that which separates, turns away). See *La Diabolie*, p. 11.

11. Note that the initiating speech makes no mention of knowledge of women. It puts off revealing the secret of the other sex and abandons the neophyte both to the enigma and the malice of women.

12. See Borch-Jacobsen's *The Freudian Subject* on the transcendence of mediation and the impracticability of imitation.

13. Meilcour's jealousy toward Hortense, his imaginary jealousy, is also mimetic in origin. He clearly perceives his torment when he believes someone else might be loved by his "unknown": "That which might refer to me might equally refer to another" (47). And elsewhere: "it was to my rival that I owed the satisfaction of seeing her look so lovely" (122).

The Power of Evil

1. Charles Baudelaire, *Œuvres complètes*, II (Paris: Gallimard, 1976), 68. The original reads: "l'énergie du mal."

2. Choderlos de Laclos, *Les Liaisons dangereuses*, trans. P. W. K. Stone (Harmondsworth: Penguin Classics, 1961), copyright P. W. K. Stone, 1961.

3. The earliest battle fought, and won, by Anton Mesmer was with Father Gassner over whether possession literally signified a diabolical parasite or else a magnetic illness to be cured by the seductive *passes* of the magnetist. See Laurence and Perry, *Hypnosis, Will, and Memory* (New York: Guilford Press, 1988), 5–23.

4. Contrary to the enlightened Merteuil, Madame de Tourvel seems indeed to regress to the earlier beliefs outlined by Michel Foucault in *The Order of Things* as characteristic of the Renaissance.

5. Quoted by Patrick Wald Lasowski, *Libertines* (Paris: Gallimard, 1980), 37.

6. Roland Barthes, *A Lover's Discourse, Fragments*, trans. Richard Howard (New York: Farrar, Straus, & Giroux, 1978), 158.

7. *Translator's note*: the French word *parasite* means both "parasite" and "static" or "interference."

8. Leibniz's monadology can be seen as a communication system that is fundamentally harmonious and perfect. The elements that make up this system (monads) have no connection with each other; only God's mediation can establish communication among the monads. The monadology thus appears as a monocentric system in which God is omnipotent and omniscient. Cf. Michel Serres, *Le Parasite* (Paris: Grasset, 1980).

9. Jean Baudrillard, *Seduction*, trans. Brian Singer (New York: St. Martin's Press, 1990), 114.

10. André Malraux, Preface to *Les Liaisons dangereuses* (Paris: Gallimard, Folio, 1970), 11.

11. We can see the punishment inflicted on Madame de Merteuil not only as vengeance wreaked by the community but also as specifically male vengeance. The Marquise is punished for her usurpation of the phallus (she attacks Prévan; she writes a letter on Valmont's behalf ending his relation with Madame de Tourvel). It is this departure from the code of permissible female behavior that becomes unacceptable. See Nancy K. Miller, *The Heroine's Text* (New York: Columbia University Press, 1980), 144–46.

12. The community seems to undertake a second purification after Madame de Merteuil's expulsion. Left in complete bankruptcy (she takes her husband's inheritance with her: diamonds, jewels, silver), the family is forced into financial reorganization.

13. Stephen Frears' film (*Dangerous Liaisons*) ends with the collapse of the universe of coquetry, with a fatal blow to Merteuil's narcissism. She is seated in front of her vanity, whose mirror shows a grim face deformed by the removal of her makeup. The director blows up her features, visibly accelerating her ruin and accentuating her moral decomposition. (In the French film adaptation of Christopher Hampton's play, Madame de Merteuil arrives at the end wrapped in a veil. With her back to the audience, the actress lifts the veil; a distorting mirror in front of her shows a face ruined by disgrace.) Likewise, in the scene at the opera, Frears finds a perfect cinematic equivalent to translate the public's condemnation of Merteuil. In Laclos's novel, she is booed by the crowd; but Frears has her stumble as she leaves her box. This *faux pas* literally scandalizes her. (*Skandalon*, a stumbling-block or trap laid in the road, and its derivative *skandalizo*,

to cause a scandal, come from the root *skazo*, "I limp.") On the adaptation of Laclos's novel for the screen, see the fine article by Alan Singerman, "Variations on a Denouement: *Les Liaisons dangereuses* on film," in *Eighteenth Century Life* 14 (1990): 53; regarding the French adaptation of Christopher Hampton's play, see the Robert Maccubin's interview with the author in the same issue.

14. Heiner Müller, *Quartet*, trans. K. Gartzke and G. Davis (Dundee, Scotland: GDR Monitor, 1984).

Gonadology

1. "To explain evil we must always return to Sade." Charles Baudelaire, *Œuvres complètes*, I (Paris: Gallimard, Pléiade, 1975), 595.

2. Donatien-Alphonse-François, Marquis de Sade, *Juliette*, trans. Austryn Wainhouse (New York: Grove/Atlantic, Inc., 1968).

3. "L'Imaginaire libertin et le corps 'spectaculeux,'" in *Revue de l'Université de Bruxelles* 3–4 (1987): 60.

4. Roland Barthes distinguishes two types of detention in the case of Sade. The first (beginning in 1763), when Sade is punished for his libertine actions (flagellation, sodomy), is segregative: "it was aimed essentially at preserving the honor of the Sade-Montreuil family"; the other (dating from 1801 to his death) is ideological and penal. Sade is detained for having written his infamous books: "it was necessary, Barthes explains, "to mobilize a subject philosophy based totally on norm and deviation." Cf. R. Barthes, *Sade, Fourier, Loyola*, 177–78.

5. M. Foucault, "Le Langage à l'infini," *Tel Quel* 15 (1963): 50.

6. For more on Sade's Leibnizian "debauchery," see Marcel Hénaff, *Sade, L'Invention du corps libertin* (Paris: Presses Universitaires de France, 1978).

7. Maurice Blanchot, "Sade," in *Justine, Philosophy in the Bedroom and Other Writings*, compiled and trans. by Richard Seaver Wainhouse (New York: Grove Weidenfeld, 1965), 59.

8. Pierre Klossowski, *Sade My Neighbor*, trans. Alphonso Lingis (Evanston, Ill.: Northwestern University Press, 1991), 100.

9. Philippe Roger understands Sadean textual pedagogy as a kind of *mimesis* (that goes so far as to affect the reader): "[the pedagogy] culminates in this extraordinary fantasy of generalized corruption, in this quantitative utopia in which appeasement is the result of engendering one's 'semblable' [one's fellow man, literally: one's *similar*]." In *Sade. La Philosophie dans le pressoir* (Paris: Grasset, 1976), 82–83.

10. Roland Barthes, *Sade, Fourier, Loyola*, trans. Richard Miller (New York: Farrar, Straus, & Giraux, 1976), 138–39.

11. Emphasis added. Sade, *La Philosophie dans le boudoir* (Paris: Union Générale d'Editions, 1972), 40–41. This quotation was adapted from Wainhouse's translation, *Justine*, 203.

12. Hénaff, *Sade*, 132.

13. *La Nouvelle Justine*, vol. 7, 47: "I will imitate her, but while hating her; I will copy her . . . but I will only do so while cursing her."

14. Cf. Hubert Damisch, "L'Ecriture sans mesures," *Tel Quel* 28 (1967), 54–56.

15. The phrase appears in French in the translation: "O Lucifer! toi que j'adore."

16. Theodor Adorno and Max Horkheimer, *Dialectic of Enlightenment*, trans. John Cumming (New York: Continuum, 1972), 94.

Deadly Quadrille

1. Johann Wolfgang von Goethe, *Elective Affinities*, trans. R. J. Hollingdale (Harmondsworth: Penguin Classics, 1971), copyright © R. J. Hollingdale, 1971.

2. *Les Affinités électives* (Paris: Gallimard Folio, 1980), 16. The reader is also referred to the masterful analysis of the novel by Tony Tanner in *Adultery in the Novel* (Baltimore: Johns Hopkins University Press, 1979), chap. 3, 179–232. On the way in which Goethe's novel presents chemistry as an art of circumstance (subject to the accidental impingement of events) rather than as a science of laws (with predictable and consistent effects), see Isabelle Stengers's remarks in "L'Affinité ambiguë: le rêve newtonien de la chimie au XVIIIe siècle," in *Eléments d'histoire des sciences*, ed. Michel Serres (Paris: Bordas, 1989), 297–319.

3. A pun in the original German: *Scheidung* means "divorce" and *Scheidekünstler* "analytical chemist."

4. "Entretiens sur les romans," in *Julie ou la nouvelle Héloïse* (Paris: Garnier-Flammarion, 1967), 42.

5. *La Transparence et l'obstacle* (Paris: Gallimard, 1971), 108.

6. *La Nouvelle Héloïse*, 42.

7. Walter Benjamin, "Les Affinités électives," in *Essais, 1, 1922–1934*, trans. Maurice de Gandillac (Paris: Denoël, 1983), 91.

8. Benjamin, "Affinités électives," 94.

9. Ibid., 104.

10. The scene of the child's conception is itself a striking enactment

of mimetic confusion. The figures of Ottilie and the captain appear in the embrace to which Charlotte and Eduard abandon themselves.

Faust

1. Johann Wolfgang von Goethe, *Faust*, trans. Philip Wayne (London: Penguin, 1949), 44.
2. Quoted by Nerval in the preface to his French translation of *Faust* (Paris: Gibert, 1878), 8.
3. Ibid.

INDEX OF NAMES

UNIVERSITY PRESS OF NEW ENGLAND publishes books under its own imprint and is the publisher for Brandeis University Press, Brown University Press, University of Connecticut, Dartmouth College, Middlebury College Press, University of New Hampshire, University of Rhode Island, Tufts University, University of Vermont, Wesleyan University Press, and Salzburg Seminar.

Library of Congress Cataloging-in-Publication Data
Saint-Amand, Pierre, 1957–
[Séduire, ou, La passion des Lumières. English]
The libertine's progress : seduction in the eighteenth-century French novel / Pierre Saint-Amand ; translated by Jennifer Curtiss Gage.
p. cm.
Includes bibliographical references and index.
ISBN 0-87451-686-2
1. French fiction—18th century—History and criticism. 2. Seduction in literature. 3. Sex in literature. I. Title.
PQ637.S43S2513 1994
843'.5093538—dc20 94-15409
∞